JAMES F. WHITE is professor of Christian worship at the Perkins School of Theology, Dallas, Texas. He is author of four books and co-author or contributor to five others, including *The Celebration of the Gospel,* published by Abingdon. He has worked on numerous interdenominational studies and has participated and lectured at various Catholic liturgical meetings. Dr. White's expertise in the field of Christian worship has been employed by numerous churches, various convocations, workshops, and convenions. As a result he has been in touch with churches throughout the country.

NEW FORMS OF WORSHIP

NEW FORMS OF WORSHIP

James F. White

Nashville • ABINGDON PRESS • New York

NEW FORMS OF WORSHIP

ISBN 0-687-27751-5

Library of Congress Catalog Card Number: 72-160797

Scripture quotations unless otherwise noted are from the Revised Standard Version of the Bible, copyrighted 1946 and 1952 by the Division of Christian Education, National Council of Churches, and are used by permission.

Excerpts from "Worship in an Age of Immediacy" by James F. White, copyright © 1968 Christian Century Foundation, are reprinted by permission from the February 21, 1968 issue of The Christian Century.

Selections from the author's article "Changing Protestant Worship: Two Revolutions in Communications" copyright © 1969 Liturgical Conference, are reprinted by permission from the June 1969 issue of Living Worship.

SET UP, PRINTED, AND BOUND BY THE PARTHENON PRESS, AT NASHVILLE, TENNESSEE, UNITED STATES OF AMERICA

For
Louise
Robert
Ellen
Laura
Martin
who
inspired and interrupted
these pages

PREFACE

This is a practical book. In a period of rapid change in the forms of worship, there seems to be a great need for a book that will give some guidance to those responsible for the planning and leadership of Christian worship. Even five years ago no one could have predicted the amount of questioning and challenge that long-established forms of worship would receive in the years that lay ahead. Nor could anyone have imagined the efforts that would be expanded in adapting Christian worship to the rapidly changing conditions of human life. In one sense, this book is a review of what has changed thus far, but it is also intended to provide guidance for those developments yet ahead of us.

It seems necessary to provide a rationale for new forms of worship. Certainly not all Christians sense the need of such changes. But it is my conviction that others feel the need for new forms of worship just as keenly as they do for new interpretations of Christian doctrine, ethics, and the biblical documents. All these must be rethought and reinterpreted for each generation. If the forms of worship have been reconsidered less frequently than doctrine, ethics, and Scripture, the work is that much more overdue. I have tried to write a rationale for new forms of worship, presenting the case for responsible reinterpretation and adaptation of the forms of Christian worship.

At the same time, I have tried to describe the direction of actual changes in worship in the early 1970s. This is definitely not a book of new services already planned that anyone can simply use. Only two complete services are described and those only as teaching experiences. I hope that the general areas of change discussed here will stimulate the imagination of others to carry the ball further down the field. The directives are general rather than specific because I am convinced that no two congregations or situations are identical. Liturgical creativity rests in the hands of ministers, priests, and lay people who know their worshiping communities. Such creativity cannot come from set formulas reproduced from books. I trust that the material in this book will provide suggestions to prime the pump of people's imaginations. The book will be a success if it provides "some help and furniture" for the leaders of worship in fulfilling their responsibilities.

Though this is a practical book, such a thing would be worse than useless unless grounded in theory. The first third of the book is an attempt to give a theoretical basis for new forms of worship. It does not take a great deal of observation to realize that much experimentation in worship has occurred without any theoretical basis and that, though the experiences may have been enjoyable, the gain has been inconsequential. The most important thing we can do here is to try to give a theoretical basis, pastorally, theologically, and historically, so that experimentation can proceed on more than a notional basis.

Some will find this theoretical basis conservative since it places a very high premium on knowledge of the past experience of Christian worship throughout the whole history of the church. I have no intention of apologizing for this conservatism. Without this kind of foundation, experimentation can only flounder around in pious subjectivism. The experiences of millions of Christians "at all times, and in all places" are much too valuable to be ignored. Unfortunately, the average leader of worship is all too ignorant of the accomplishments of two thousand years of experimentation in Christian worship. So I am deliberately and unapologetically conservative in this respect.

On the other hand, I recognize that much that appears in these pages will soon be dated. This book was written in 1969 and 1970 for the early 1970s. I hope and trust that the theoretical parts will have a continuing validity, but I expect much of the more practical portions will be obsolete in five years' time. During the time from 1966 to 1976 our work seems to be to reflect what the electronic media have done to people. After 1976, we can expect the extensive use of the new electronic media in worship itself. That gives us maybe five years before these media affect worship in most churches. We have much to learn and even more to unlearn in the meantime. So this book is meant to be used in the first half of the 1970s and after that time will be a small bit of history itself. This may seem like a short life expectancy for a book, but it is all one can hope for in a time of such rapid change. In the meantime, we have much learning to do, much to catch up with in a very short time.

I have directed myself to an audience of ministers, priests, and lay members of worship committees. I rejoice that we live in an age when Protestants and Catholics have learned so much from each other. I only hope that we do not have to make each other's mistakes but can profit from knowing what not to do as well as what is worth doing. At any rate, this book is meant to be a contribution to the ecumenical age of the church. I write, and this may or may not be obvious, as a minister of The United Methodist Church and as a professor of worship in a United Methodist seminary. Some of the examples may have a Methodist flavor, but I think for the most part my denominational background is inconspicuous. At any rate, I have tried to speak to all Christians, though one never quite fully grasps just how much his perspectives and assumptions are determined by his own station in life.

I should point out that several of the examples and experiments described have taken place in Perkins Chapel of Perkins School of Theology, Southern Methodist University, Dallas, Texas. The congregation has been that of Protestant seminarians, the people I know best. Since I am convinced that experimentation has to be conducted in the context of specific people, places, and times, I do not apologize that much of what I describe has been in one specific situation. I have frequently been obliged to plan and lead innovative services in the Southwest and in many other parts of the country under widely varying circumstances with different types of congregations. I never relish these roadshow demands and hence make little reference to them since the people and places have been unfamiliar to me. Instead, I have particularized by referring to the people and place I do know and trust my readers will do likewise. Generalized experiments and discussions have little to commend them since each congregation and situation is unique. When it comes to worship, I try to take situation and context with utmost seriousness though operating with certain guiding norms.

Perkins Chapel has been a good laboratory since it presents most of the problems of an attractive, expensive, and absolutely rigid neo-Georgian building of the 1950s. It seats 451 people. The Chapel presents most of the problems found in virtually all the churches built before the 1950s and in all too many of those erected since. A more flexible building would have been less challenging but also far less representative of the great majority of American churches. It should be remembered that the worship offered in this context has not been clinical but part of the scheduled worship life of the seminary community.

It is a pleasure to give thanks for and to the library staffs of two institutions with outstanding collections in the area of liturgy. Mr. Decherd H. Turner, Jr., and the entire staff of Bridwell Library of Perkins School of Theology have always been most gracious in every way in securing books and answering my queries. The staff of the Alcuin Library at St. John's University, Collegeville, Minnesota, have also been most generous. Not only did they provide me with an office where the major portion of this book was written, but they extended countless courtesies. They proved that monastic hospitality is alive and well. Much of this book developed from lectures I gave during the 1969 Summer School of Theology at McGill University. I am indebted to Professor John C. Kirby for his invitation to give these lectures and for his many kindnesses during my stay in Montreal.

I have profited greatly from the comments of many of my colleagues who read portions of the manuscript, particularly Professors Leroy T. Howe, Decherd H. Turner, Jr., Joe R. Jones, and Carlton R. Young. The comments of the Reverend Robert E. Allen, Mr. John F. Erickson, and the Reverend John Gallen, S.J., have led to numerous improvements. Professor H. Grady Hardin read the entire manuscript and his suggestions are reflected on many pages of this book. Mrs. John Norris and Mrs. Vella Massey survived the task of deciphering my manuscript and produced clarity and light out of my murky manuscript.

Only an author knows how indebted he is to his wife for all the allowances she makes for the things he does not do and all the help she provides in doing things for him while he is writing. To our children, to whom this book is dedicated, I apologize for all the months of neglect that it has meant and only hope that the time was used for an even greater good.

December 30, 1970
JAMES F. WHITE

CONTENTS

I

ON STARTING WITH PEOPLE

Something extraordinary happened to Christian worship in the late 1960s. Even the secular press noticed the change and began to carry articles about worship. The very fact that Christian worship had become newsworthy was in itself significant, for newspapers and magazines were not providing their readers with the usual Monday-morning sermon outlines. They were reporting on the whole worship service often described as "experimental" or "innovative" and hardly bothering to mention the sermon. What "he said" had been superseded by accounts of what "they did." The year 1966 marks approximately the beginning of public notice that something basic was changing in the forms of Christian worship. The press, of course, found that the strange and unfamiliar made better news copy than worship as usual and doubtlessly was inclined to exaggerate the prevalence of change. But clearly something new and significant was beginning in the forms of Christian worship.

This is all the more strange if one recalls the dominant currents visible in Protestant worship in the early 1960s. It was a time, we may remember, of the recovery of Reformation patterns of worship. Both the legacy of neo-orthodox theology and the contributions of serious historical scholarship had produced a new fascination with the liturgies of the Reformation. There was much talk about recovering our heritage in worship, and this generally meant a new appreciation of Reformation liturgies from Martin Luther's *Formula Missae* of 1523 to John Knox's *The Forme of Prayers* of 1556. For Methodists it might be extended as far as John Wesley's *Sunday Service* of 1784, and some even felt that Philip Schaff's (and others) *Order of Worship* of 1866 deserved a second look. The process of liturgical revision was moving in the direction of recovering practices promoted by the sixteenth-century Reformers. While the Methodist *Book of Worship* was being revised prior to 1964, it was seriously proposed that the communion order be a return to Thomas Cranmer's 1549 service, leapfrogging over the subsequent revisions. To a certain extent this is what was actually done. The Methodist revisers, like all others of that time, retained the familiar sixteenth-century English prose.

Within five years such procedures had been forsaken altogether by denominations revising their service books. If they looked to the past it was not so much to the Reformation as to the early church that they turned. And no one seriously considered sixteenth-century English as acceptable for a new service book. Instead, denominations vied with one another to create a "contemporary" liturgical prose.

There are various reasons for such a shift. One of the most obvious is the corresponding change in Roman Catholic worship. The *Constitution on the Sacred Liturgy,* formally promulgated on December 4, 1963, and the first *Instruction for the Proper Implementation of the Constitution* issued the following September, set the pattern for a thorough revision of liturgical books. Since then, the appearance of new instructions, the successive publication of each new *editio typica* of the liturgical books, and the subsequent translations into many languages have produced far-reaching changes in Catholic worship. Those impatient with the official rate of change have gone further and faster though sometimes forced to do so in underground gatherings. Many of these "underground" services seem better publicized than normal parish masses and have helped to speed up the rate of change within Protestantism too.

Another factor lies in the cycles of religious boom and depression. The 1950s were a period of religious boom in America just as the 1930s had seen a religious depression as well as the economic one. By the late 1960s a considerable decline in church attendance became evident. According to Gallup poll figures, there was a drop from a high of 49 percent of the adult population attending church during a typical week in 1958 to 42 percent in 1969. Even more significant was the decline in the same eleven years in the percentage of young adults (ages 21-29) attending church, a drop from 48 percent to 33 percent.[1] Compared to many other nations these figures remain very high but they do indicate a trend that few American churchmen could fail to notice with concern. Church attendance patterns certainly stimulated attempts to find new forms of worship.

But when all is said and done, these religious factors pale in significance with others. Those are the changes that were becoming apparent in people themselves. Changes in church law, theology, and attendance are important but they can hardly account for the experimentation in worship so common in the late 1960s. We have to look deeper. What was happening to people in those years? How were the conditions of American life changing? How were people themselves changing? These are the questions we must probe in order to understand the efforts to achieve new forms of worship.

I

Anyone with eyes open recognizes that American life has changed drastically in the last few years. We can only note here the most obvious elements of change, particularly those that have direct impact on the way American Christians understand and practice worship.

The most distinctive shift in American life in the last few years, it seems to me, has been the splintering of society. Whereas only a few years back it was taken for granted that American society would have a basic agreement on the life style, morality, and range of acceptable opinions appropriate to its members, this unanimity is today shattered. That the style of life congenial to forty-year-old middle-class whites was to be normative for all society has been rudely questioned and found wanting by many elements of society which once submitted to such forms, however alien to them. The splintering of society has ended the superficial homogeneity of American

---

[1] Figures by permission of George Gallup, Jr., president of the American Institute of Public Opinion, Princeton, New Jersey.

life by cracking the thin shell of conformity under which so much of life had been ordered.

The consequence has been a radically new development in freedom for many though questioned vigorously by the majority. It can be argued that despite tremendous pressures for conformity, there are greater possibilities for freedom, for "doing one's own thing," than at any time in our nation's past since the closing of the frontier. It may well be that the greatest achievement of our time has been the assertion of peoples' duty to be true to themselves rather than conforming to the mold society had prepared for them.

This new freedom appears in many different aspects of American life. Most obvious is the emergence of different life styles, some of them completely foreign to our past. The 1969 movie, *Easy Rider,* portrays at least five quite distinct life styles: those of two itinerant motorcyclists, a farm family, a hippie commune, a small-town lawyer, and small-town people in southern America. In the film, those with these distinct life styles have little in common and often show mutual hostility. It is in many ways a good mirror of American life at the beginning of the 1970s. Many more possible life styles are open to us today than was the case a decade ago. There are, at last, alternatives to being a middle-class suburban home owner.

The possibility of alternative life styles is not simply a matter of age, though those under thirty seem to have taken more advantage of the choices. At every age, young or old, there are those who relish or anticipate a life of home ownership, mowing the grass, and rearing their children in physical comfort. But one's choice to reject suburban values of security and comfort is more apt to be accepted, if not comprehended, by society today than in the recent past. The splintering of society has made different life styles present possibilities and not just dreams.

The same is true of moralities. Prohibition was probably the last great effort to standardize patterns of morality in America. Most Christians have come to accept the possibility of other people living conscientious Christian lives with the moderate use of alcohol even though they may not drink themselves. There seem to be some signs that the same thing is happening with regard to the use of nonnarcotic drugs. Most of the population may avoid them completely, but they may eventually accept the use of some drugs as an acceptable pattern of behavior. Homosexuality has become increasingly recognized as a possible form of sexuality for those so disposed who do not interfere with others. And premarital sex causes little stir in much of our society.

Yet side by side remains a large section of the population which rejects the use of alcohol, drugs, homosexuality, or premarital sex. Society seems less apt to condemn those who condone these practices partly because these same persons are often more morally rigorous in their condemnation of militarism, racism, marriage for money, and avarice. Who is to say who is more moral? In a system of pluralistic moralities there is less and less consensus as to what is right and wrong. People with quite opposing concepts of morality are more and more prone to accept and even respect those whose moral codes they dislike.

Not long ago we thought that the goal for black people was to emulate the patterns of white America. Today many black people have found a cultural identity that is no longer a mirror reflection of white culture. Our efforts to make the Indians over in our own image now appears to be a flagrantly misguided effort. Nor do Mexican-Americans find it a step forward to forget their past. Why we once prided ourselves on being a melting pot, on losing our identities in one vast flux, seems puzzling. Being black, being Indian or Mexican-American can now mean having found authenticity in one's own blackness or whatever it be that separates him from the dominant majority. Pride has come to be a virtue for many to whom our society once denied such a sense of self-confidence.

The generation gap has been highly publicized though this is nothing new. There has always been a gap between generations, otherwise the process of accumulating experiences would add up to very little. But there do seem to be two things that make the present generation gap of great significance. The first thing is that we accept, expect, and talk about it. It is something new that the generation gap should be an important element of national discussion instead of something to be ashamed of by those who could not make their children conform. The acceptance of this inevitability of disjuncture between children and parents is a major step toward greater freedom within society.

There is also the factor that those growing up in America since World War II have experienced such a constant element of change that change has become one of the givens in their expectations of life itself. The only certainty in life today seems to be that the rate of change will accelerate and even that may change! No longer does it seem the least bit likely that children will live in the same conditions as their parents though that was once a reasonable expectation. Becoming accustomed to change as a way of life is an important factor in the generation gap itself. Children are different today because they expect change as about the only thing they can count on in life, something far less certain for previous generations.

Out of the splintering of society, we argue, have come great benefits in making it possible for people to be more true to themselves. Unfortunately, we do not give up old standards and behavior patterns easily and the new freedom within society has produced many tensions and antagonisms. Many of the changes have come about by forcible confrontations rather than by mutual tolerance. American society is deeply wounded by conflicts between those who champion new practices and those who resist giving up what has been valid for them. Arrogance abounds on every side. But even the harshness of the conflicts should not blind us to that which is emerging—a grudging acceptance that different life styles, parallel moralities, and generation gaps may each be valid in terms of the people whom they reflect. We are finally realizing that pluralism goes far deeper than mere toleration of different varieties of Christianity or of an assortment of European nationalities.

The new freedom is worth all the present-day conflicts and more. It is no longer necessary for everyone to submerge himself to the mainstream of American life. He can "cop out"; he has an alternative, indeed, several. As our society becomes increasingly complex, so does the range of possibilities expand. We have choices our fathers could not make. We can express what it means to be us, whether we be "square" or radical. Polonius' rhetoric now makes more sense than it did to Laertes: "This above all: to thine own self be true." We can be so more nearly today as long as it does not interfere with similar privileges for others.

Of course it is by no means simply a matter of age groups. Within every age level there are great varieties of people now free to be themselves. This has tremendous consequences for Protestant worship. For our worship has been oriented to one particular type of person within the large white denominations. Our services reflect the values, modes of perceiving reality, and life styles with which a forty-year-old middle-class white person feels familiar, especially one with a college education. For him the forms of Protestant worship seem natural and normal. Until recently we could force everyone else to fit this pattern too. Fortunately this is no longer possible nor feasible. We can no longer say, "Like it or lump it." There is another alternative; they can leave. And many have.

There are good reasons why the forms of Protestant worship seem so natural and normal to many of those in the pews and equally good reasons why these same forms seem so alien and unnatural to others of our contemporaries. We shall have to take a brief historical excursion in order to understand the present better.

II

The shape of present-day Protestant worship is largely a consequence of the communications revolution of the fifteenth and sixteenth centuries. The Reformation coincided with one of the greatest communications revolutions of all time—the invention of the cheap book. The combination of this revolution and the theological revolution of the Reformation shaped Protestant worship for four hundred years.

Christian worship had known the use of written formularies from at least the third century. Hippolytus' liturgy, which dates from the early third century, presents a written form of prayer, though he testifies to elasticity in his provision that bishops may improvise. Serapion's prayerbook from the fourth century is further evidence of the use of written texts, and from that time onward the use of written rites is clear. Even so, it was only the clergy who had a missal, a ritual, or whatever service book was needed. The very terms "cleric" or "clerk" often referred to someone who could read and write, since the average layman was illiterate or "lewd," i.e. nonclerical.

In the Middle Ages, books were used by the clergy, but what they had to say in the mass, apart from the sermon, was usually hard to hear and even harder to understand for those who did not know Latin. The priest was the man with the book, and he was the only one who could "say" mass. For most people, both the culture and worship were preliterate. People participated at mass largely by watching the actions of the priest at the altar. The laity had few, if any, words to offer in their worship. Stephen Gardiner, Catholic bishop of Winchester, England, wrote in 1547:

> It was never meant that the people should indeed hear the Matins or hear the Mass, but be present there and pray themselves in silence; with common credit to the priests and clerks, that although they hear not a distinct sound to know what they say, yet to judge that they for their part were and be well occupied, and in prayer; and so should they be.[2]

The laity were to keep quiet and occupy themselves with their own private devotions.

Gutenberg changed all that though not in the most obvious way. His invention, of course, was a means of mass-producing books. Books, formerly possessions only of clergy and men of wealth, could be mass produced after the 1450s with each printed page being identical with all others from the same type.[3] At last books could be sold cheaply. Tyndale's hope that his biblical translations could be read by "a boy that driveth the plough" was possible only in a print culture. The 1549 *Book of Common Prayer* was limited in price by royal authority to no more than two shillings two pence unbound.[4]

But the most important result of the invention of printing was not that in the course of more than a century books be-

[2] *The Letters of Stephen Gardiner,* ed. by James A. Muller (New York: The Macmillan Co., 1933), p. 355. Spelling modernized.

[3] Marshall McLuhan, *The Gutenberg Galaxy, The Making of Typographic Man* (Toronto: University of Toronto Press, 1967), p. 125.

[4] Henry Barclay Swete, *Church Services and Service Books Before the Reformation* (London: S.P.C.K., 1930), p. 10 n.

came available to most people. <u>What matters most is what</u> <u>reading did to people</u>. Learning to read does things to people as can be observed by watching any first-grade school child. Reading is an individual act. You need no one to do it for you. The child stops demanding, "tell me a story," and goes into a corner to read by himself. What he learns does not come through a person but through little splotches of black ink pressed into a white page. Reading is a solitary act; we put up quiet signs in libraries. It is also depersonalized, since things communicate to us rather than people. And consequently reading is more likely to stimulate the intellect than the emotions. It is hard to get quite as excited about what ink and paper say to us compared to what flesh and blood say when we are confronted by a living human. Only one medium communicates to us in print, rather than the multiplicity of voice, facial expressions, and gestures of a human being. In reading we are accustomed to reality being mediated to us through a single and impersonal medium, the printed page.

There is another important consequence which Marshall McLuhan called "the linear structuring of rational life of phonetic literacy." [5] The printed page metes out information in a neat orderly sequence, word after word, line after line. One thing comes at a time. Instead of the instantaneous impact of meeting a person and seeing and hearing him at the same time, we read about these one item at a time. So the reader becomes doubly detached from the reality the book describes. Reality is mediated through cold print and in a sequential and linear pattern rather than instantaneously.

<u>The invention of printing drastically changed people and the</u> <u>ways they perceived reality.</u> Reading heightened their individualistic self-reliance. It also pushed them to approach reality in terms of sequential analysis, taking things in an orderly fashion. At the same time, the senses of taste, touch, and smell, instantaneous in impact and completely absent from printing, were eclipsed. The importance of printing for Protestant worship lies much more in what it did to people than in the mechanical possibilities that it opened up for the conduct of services. <u>People had changed and the Reformers could</u>

[5] *Understanding Media: The Extensions of Man* (New York: Signet Books, 1966), p. 87.

make a new start in worship because they were dealing with a new kind of person, literate man.

All this had tremendous consequences for the shaping of Protestant worship. Indeed, in some areas it may have overcome the theological preferences of the Reformers themselves. One of the great accomplishments of the Reformers with regard to worship was that they seemed to grasp what was happening to people in northern Europe and the opportunities these changes presented for renewing the forms of worship. In part it was a chain reaction just as the introduction of the vernacular has been in Roman Catholic worship in our own time. The Reformers differed in how far they followed out the consequences of the print revolution, the churches of the Reformed tradition being the most consistent in shaping their worship around the new emphasis on the word.

The first and most obvious consequence of a literate laity was that they could participate verbally in services of worship in a much fuller way. No longer were they restricted to litanies and those few phrases that memory could recover. Hymns, prayers, lections, psalms now became accessible to them. The clerical monopoly was broken, for now all could be clerics, i.e., readers. Gutenberg made possible in worship what Luther proclaimed about the priesthood of all believers. The result was a raising of the status of the laity rather than a lowering of the clergy.

But there were other effects. The laity, for the most part, read their native tongues, not Latin. Luther began by preparing a Latin liturgy. But for most people a book in Latin was no better than none. Others preceded Luther in enabling a literate laity to participate in worship through vernacular translations. Soon all important Protestant leaders recognized this necessity though themselves fluent in Latin. The language of the laity was adopted in every land of the Reformation. Since any translation expresses ideas in new forms and thus subtly changes those same concepts, translation was the crucial act in shaping each Protestant tradition of worship. Even the most careful translation is couched in the new language into which the ideas are rendered, and thus the various liturgies adopted the thought patterns of sixteenth-century German, French, Dutch, English, and other languages.

It was also evident that drastic simplification would be necessary for the laity to participate verbally in the service. Cranmer's complaint in 1549 with regard to the old service books: "That many times, there was more busines to fynd out what should be read, then to read it when it was founde out" [6] led to considerable pruning and simplification. His prayer book distilled into one volume the contents of the missal, breviary, ritual, and pontifical and put it all into the hands of the laity. A Bible was the only other book necessary for the conduct of the services of the Church of England. Simplification, then, was a keynote of Protestant worship, achieved largely by subtraction rather than new additions.

Worship for Protestants came to be expressed primarily through two mediums, the word spoken and the word read. It is no accident that the biblical image of the "Word of God" came to be so important. Whether identified with Christ himself, Scripture, preaching, or inward perception, the "Word of God" remains the most conspicuous image of the Reformation. The Puritans treated the Bible itself as a book of canons as to what was suitable for worship, reformed according to God's Word.

The preaching of the Word of God came to occupy the longest time of any part of public worship. Luther felt that the congregation "should never gather together without the preaching of God's Word and prayer." [7] In much of Protestantism even the prayers eventually took on the nature of brief homilies, and the whole service seemed to be a frame for the sermon. Hourglasses were placed in many English churches to measure the length of the sermon. God's Word was not just expounded; it was expounded fully and frequently.

A good indication of what was happening is provided in the fate of the church year. Many of the Reformers were convinced that all Scripture was written for man's instruction (Romans 15:4), hence lectionaries based on the calendar were scrapped for a *lectio continua* in which one plodded through whole books of the Bible instead of reading the appropriate

[6] "The Preface" to 1549 *Book of Common Prayer, The First and Second Prayer Books of Edward VI* (London: J. M. Dent & Sons, 1952), p. 4.
[7] "Concerning the Order of Public Worship," *Luther's Works* (Philadelphia: Fortress Press, 1965), LIII:11.

selections for special days and seasons of the calendar. None of God's Word was neglected, but the peaks and valleys of the church year were leveled to a flat plain of continuous reading.

A linear mentality had come to dominate man. It often worked contrary to the desires of the Reformers. Luther, Calvin, and Cranmer desired that the main Sunday service be the Lord's Supper as it had been since New Testament times. But in each case their wishes were frustrated. Instead, the service of the Word from the Lord's Supper or the pattern of the divine office (based on the Scriptures, psalms, and prayer) ousted the full Lord's Supper from dominance. In effect, the synagogue triumphed over the upper room.

The causes of this great change in the main diet of congregational worship (undoubtedly the greatest transformation in Reformation worship though neither desired nor anticipated by many of the Reformers) was largely due to what had happened to man. The communications impact of the Lord's Supper is instantaneous. In one service is represented the very heart of the gospel: Christ's passion, death, and resurrection. The impact of the divine office and the service of the Word, on the other hand, is cumulative. Bits of salvation history are commemorated week after week in lessons, psalms, hymns, and sermons. In the course of time these add up to the whole gospel, but the approach is basically one item at a time in a steady progression, week after week. Nothing could be better suited to the mentality of literate man, for he looks at reality in a linear and sequential fashion. Thus the pattern of the divine office or service of the Word became his most natural form of worship. The Lord's Supper became an occasional ceremony, eventually celebrated only three times a year in the Church of England or quarterly in the Church of Scotland. The triumph of the linear mentality was complete.

For Protestants, worship came to be equated with the reading, singing, and speaking of words. "Reading prayers," or "going to the sermon" came to be Protestant ways of speaking of worship. In short, the ethos of Protestant worship came to be bookish just as did the culture of Protestant regions. Unfortunately, the great stress on the word read, sung, and spoken led to corresponding losses in other areas. The whole vocabulary of gestures that had been so important in medieval worship was sloughed off. The Puritans denounced many bits of ceremonial as "popish abuses" and "badges of Antichrist" unless "gathered out of the word of God." But it may be equally significant that the Protestant emphasis on verbalization made them superfluous. The visual arts withered away, and Protestant worship became, for all purposes, color-blind. Color was as absent from churches as from the printed page. Vestments disappeared except in Sweden to be replaced by conservative black street dress or professors' gowns. Sir Christopher Wren designed his churches by calculating the optimum distance that a preacher's voice could be heard and referred to Protestant church buildings as "to be fitted for Auditories." To be sure, his buildings did employ bits of baroque carving as adornment, and the New England meetinghouses were often painted colors until the Greek revival of the nineteenth century whitened them all. But none of this adornment could properly be called liturgical art, nor did it bear any intrinsic relationship to the building's function in worship.

Sixteenth-century Protestant worship, then, was shaped by the same forces that were shaping men at the time, especially by the new development of widespread literacy. The forms of worship became those most natural to the people of the time. Catholicism, on the other hand, made little acknowledgment of what was happening to men except to seize the possibility of standardizing liturgical texts. A variety of local uses still survived, but these were abolished (with few exceptions) at the advent of printing. The Roman breviary of 1568, the missal of 1570, and subsequent books led the way to a standardization of texts no matter in what part of the world the divine office or mass was said. Mass-produced books led to identical rites. Protestantism succumbed to the same temptation, and various acts of uniformity provided for one identical prayer book in England and Wales so that "all the whole realme shall haue but one use." Catholicism managed to ignore the consequences of Gutenberg's revolution except for accomplishing the standardization of texts.

Protestantism allowed people to worship in the forms most natural to them. This has been the strength of Protestant worship for more than four hundred years. There were, of course, occasional variations. On the American frontier, where literacy could not be taken for granted, some quite divergent forms of worship developed. They made more use of the emotions and stressed various gestures through use of the sawdust trail, the mourner's bench, and the altar call. Similar features tended to be characteristic in the black churches.

A further development considerably affected Protestant worship though not mentioned in any liturgical textbooks. In 1884 a Chicago businessman, A. B. Dick, solved a business need for rapid duplication by inventing a process for stencil duplication. It proved so efficient that he marketed it under the name of "Mimeograph." Gutenberg made it possible to put prayer books in the hands of people; Dick made prayer books obsolete. Prayer books are mostly propers which are hard to locate and confusing to most people. Dick gave each minister his own printing press and a new possibility of printing only what was needed on any specific occasion. Xerox and other processes promise to do the same for hymnals. These developments have simply completed what Gutenberg began, and in worship as elsewhere we are now flooded with printed paper.

III

Protestant worship, then, was shaped by the communications and theological revolutions of the sixteenth century and made creative use of what had happened to man. Basically these premises remained valid until very recently when we find ourselves in the midst of an equally tremendous new communications revolution, a similar theological one having already occurred in the accommodation of religion to scientific discoveries. The new communications revolution is much more impatient than its predecessor. It has not required a hundred years or more to affect whole populations. Technology has provided a variety of new media and, even more significant, has made them available cheaply. Television, the most conspicuous of the new media, has not turned out to be a luxury of the privileged few (like medieval books) but a necessity of the masses. Its importance, like printed books, lies in the fact that it knows no élite.

This new communications revolution has happened to us so fast that we are hardly aware of its effects on us. We still judge it in terms of our past, putting movies on television just as we made movies out of books. Yet the great importance of what television (along with the telephone, speed in travel, and other new possibilities) has done for us is often ignored when it is seen just as an alternate way of presenting the same information. That is to miss the point altogether. Marshall McLuhan has argued that the medium itself is the message and we must perceive what the new media do to us, not just the message that they present.[8] Our thesis here is that the new media, especially television, have caused a drastic change in our means of perceiving reality, just as the advent of mass literacy did in the sixteenth century. This is particularly true of those who have grown up on television. Since half of the American population has been born since World War II, that includes vast numbers of people. In 1954, for the first time, television surpassed radio in the amount of broadcast revenues it produced.

Television plugs each of us into the events of the whole world. McLuhan has popularized the phrase, "the global village."[9] It is as if we all once again were squatted around a tribal campfire, taking part in whatever was happening to the tribe. But that tribe is now world-wide. Instead of the perimeter of the village campfire being our widest horizon, we now find ourselves elbow to elbow with the whole human race. When man first stepped on the moon, it is estimated that one fifth of the human race saw him do so. In a very real sense we were all there.

It is this quality of being a direct participant in the event which makes television so different from reading. One reads about an event, seeing it through the eyes of the writer. In television he sees it happen directly with his own eyes. The old phrase, "seeing is believing," describes the television event. But television excites more than just eyesight since the sense of touch is so closely related to seeing. Affected is the sense of touch as well as hearing and seeing. Television involves the

[8] Marshall McLuhan, *Understanding Media*, p. 24.
[9] Marshall McLuhan and Quentin Fiore, *War and Peace in the Global Village* (New York: Bantam Books, 1968).

emotions too. One reacts directly to what he sees and hears, not to something described by a writer. So our emotions and our senses of touch, hearing, and seeing are all sucked into the television event.

Television demands a much greater degree of participation than reading or radio since several senses work simultaneously. We become part of the event. No one could have watched the riots at the 1968 Democratic Convention in Chicago and remained neutral. One had to take sides, either with the youth or the police. The same event, printed in the newspapers the next day, could be analyzed without passion or commitment. The detached act of reading about such an event was a completely different experience of its reality from that of being there via television. A medium such as television demands our full involvement for we become a part of the action. We do not remain passive, analytical, noninvolved.

Television's impact on us is instantaneous. Partly because the value of broadcast seconds is measured in thousands of dollars, television works on compression, leaving us much to fill in ourselves. A television program compresses into half an hour or an hour a story that the more leisurely medium of the movies loiters over for double that time. We do not have to rely on an author to set the setting. It's there; we see it immediately. A whole variety of circumstances can be grasped from a few short glimpses, or they can even be superimposed on one another.

Part of the problem with television is that it is still a new medium for those of us over thirty. Our children never knew a world without television. They start watching it long before they learn to read. They see, it has been calculated, about fifteen thousand hours of television before they reach eighteen. During the same years they have been in the classroom about 10,800 hours.[10] The child who once had to wait till he was six to learn to read and thus to expand his horizon beyond those near him now accomplishes the same by the flick of a switch. Furthermore, it is often just as much entertainment as it is education. Parents rarely have to force their children to watch television. The same can hardly be said with regard to reading!

[10] B. F. Jackson, ed., Communication—Learning for Churchmen (Nashville: Abingdon Press, 1968) p. 72.

Those under twenty-five have grown up with different modes of perceiving reality than their parents. We older people expect information to be supplied us in the sequential forms of print. We read about Guadalcanal the day after. Our children see war in Vietnam as it happens. We grew up on media where everything was spelled out for us. Our children see for themselves. There is no need to reduce events to words when they are participants via television. And so their methods of perceiving reality are quite different from those of their parents who grew up under quite different circumstances.

In some ways our children are like men before the invention of printing when information had to be communicated to the illiterate through other persons or at least through visual representations on the walls of churches and in the market. They are sensitive to many forms of sensory input, and their basic orientation is to the immediate and instantaneous rather than to the linear and sequential. McLuhan calls the "now" generation "post-literate." It has come to perceive reality through the immediacy of direct experience.

Small wonder then that we have problems with our forms of worship. The forms most natural for perceiving reality on the part of the youth do not coincide with those of the older adult. Several national magazines failed to attract younger readers and their eventual demise should be a word of warning to the church. Worship in the main-line white churches still consists almost entirely of a diet of words spooned out to us by the minister. We adults prefer to be nourished this way, but the youth feel underfed. We adults are largely oriented to verbal forms of perception, since we have been watching television for fewer years than we have been reading. The question we still ask when we miss church is, "What did he say?"—meaning, "What was the sermon about?" The younger generation is more likely to ask, "What happened?" For them the problem is that nothing happened, or at least very little and much of that was insignificant. The congregation stood, sang a few hymns, and went home.

By and large, Protestant worship is still in the realm of the communications revolution of the sixteenth century. After four hundred and fifty years the times have changed, most of all within the last twenty years. We must realize that people have changed. They are accustomed to much more immediate forms of communication than words read from a book. And consequently the forms by which worship is expressed must change too.

IV

To say that there is an imperative for changes in the forms of worship, at least for some people, does not indicate what those changes should be. We can approach this problem on a theoretical level by establishing norms by which forms of worship can be evaluated. Then, in chapters four through nine, we shall discuss specific parts of worship.

Three norms seem to be crucial in evaluating any form of worship, old or new. The first of these we have been considering in this chapter—the forms of worship must be natural to the perceptual and expressive character of the worshipers. This we may call the *pastoral norm:* the forms of worship should reflect the people who worship. In the next chapter we shall discuss a *theological norm:* the forms must express Christian faith. Then we shall expound a *historical norm:* we must learn from those forms which have functioned well in expressing Christian worship in the past.

In essence, we have been discussing the present crisis in terms of the pastoral norm throughout this chapter, but a few specific comments at this point may prove helpful. The chief brunt of the pastoral norm is the need for a minister to know his people. It is no accident that the cutting edge in liturgical studies today seems to be in sociology, anthropology, and communications theory. What we do not know in these areas will hurt us.

The day of universal liturgical reform is past. *The Constitution on the Sacred Liturgy* acknowledged the need to respect and foster "the spiritual adornments and gifts of various races and peoples." [11] The "in" word is "indigenization." The issues of *Notitiae,* the organ of the Consilium for the Implementation of the Constitution on the Sacred Liturgy, are replete

---

[11] Walter M. Abbott, S.J., ed., *The Documents of Vatican II* (New York: Guild Press, America Press, and Association Press, 1966), p. 151.

in requests from different parts of the world for variations in the mass and other rites. The *agnus dei* proved offensive when translated in parts of India, the baptismal ceremonies were misconstrued in Africa, liturgical colors produced different responses in parts of the world where white might be associated with mourning or red with weddings.

Even more so do we need to become sensitive to the various subcultures within any given culture. The type of worship emanating from a youth culture and described in *Multi-Media Worship*[12] proved to be most offensive to many outside that age group when telecast nationally. It was natural in one situation, it was outrageous in others. The experience is familiar. Anyone who is asked to "come and do an experimental service" soon realizes how impossible this is without a knowledge of the people who will be worshiping. Only a pastor who knows his people can effectively introduce and nurture new forms of worship that are authentic expressions of his people.

The splintering of society means that to be true and relevant to people as they now are, we will need to be all things to all people. In the past we have offered what businessmen call a manufacturing mentality. We produced a product and then looked for someone to take it. Now, instead, we need a marketing mentality. Businesses operating on a manufacturing mentality are not apt to survive since their competitors can produce something that people really want. Yet such has been the mentality of the church. A marketing mentality searches for what people want and need and then resolves to satisfy that need. Our pastoral norm emphasizes the need to recognize the great variety of persons in the church today and their varying conditions of life. This almost automatically demands a greater number of choices of types of worship. Henry Ford is reputed to have promised the customer any color as long as it was black, but Ford Motor Company would not be in business today if it had kept that policy.

One of the obvious consequences of acceptance of the generation gap as inevitable and healthy is the divisiveness it produces within the family. It has become increasingly diffi

[12] Edited by Myron Bloy (New York: Seabury Press, 1969).

cult for members of the same family to find things that they enjoy doing in common. We take it for granted that the family will receive its education with peer groups. We have become accustomed to each age group in the family finding its own form of recreation. When children become teen-agers they practically have to be coerced to take their recreation with their parents. The appeal of the peer group in establishing fashions, makeup, taste in music, favorite television programs, and almost everything else is extremely hard to resist. It even becomes a struggle to force the family to eat together at the same time despite the advantage (to the parents) of this opportunity for passing laws!

It then seems a bit romantic and quaint to argue that at least the family ought to worship together. If they do little else together, is it not a bit unnatural to make worship the exception? We may not like what is happening to the family, but we can ill afford to ignore these effects. Why should we demand that little children "sit still during church" when everyone knows that nowhere else do little children sit still? We long ago gave up using the same educational methods and subjects with every age group. Why should we expect the same forms of worship to be normative for each age within the family?

Our worship must be constructed around a healthy respect for the varieties of people who will be worshiping either in homogeneous or heterogeneous groups. What is appropriate worship for children may not be so for teen-agers or for their parents. No longer can we afford to offer a menu with only one dinner on it. For years we have, in effect, said: "This is it and you can take it or leave it."

We ministers are often hardly aware of how arrogant our presuppositions with regard to worship have been. We knew what was good for people, and that we gave them. Nowhere is this more evident than with regard to church music. We wanted "good" music, so schools of sacred music flourished to train musicians who would see that the church got the best. It might not be the music that the congregation would sing. It might not be the music that was represented in their record collections at home. But at least it fitted our standards of classical good taste.

Rarely did we stop to consider how arbitrary our actions were. Can we any longer defend such aesthetic snobbery? I personally may prefer not to listen to church music past Mozart and Haydn. But what right do I have to enforce such preferences on a congregation? Unfortunately, we often thought we were doing the congregation a favor by imposing standards of quality on them. Too often this concern for "quality" as determined by past artistic forms has been more "symbolic of a snob church for an élite than a part of the culture of the masses." [13] Few present-day clergy realize just how classical the presuppositions of their education have been or how rigid and inflexible their mentality is. And this applies to far more than church music. Perhaps this is philistinism, but maybe the alternative has too long been an aesthetic snobbery that is no more defensible. Our knowing what is best for congregations needs to be based on more than those standards of good taste that we learned years ago in seminary. Perhaps the people know what is best for them and we ought to take them into our confidence. The Roman Catholic Consilium on the Liturgy had two laymen (both church musicians) and one lay woman and a couple of hundred clerical consultors. Yet the Catholic Church is more than ninety-nine per-cent laity. Most other denominations do not do much better, and the imbalance is often found even on commissions on worship in the local church.

We need, then, to accept people and the forms of perception and expression most natural to them, not to prescribe them. It should be pointed out that the forms of communication are theologically ambiguous. A verbal form of expression is neither more nor less Christian than a visual one. Indeed all forms are inherently secular since they have been taken from normal forms of human intercourse. Only long association has given religious connotations. Organ music is considered churchly in the West, associated with taverns in the East. The mass is just as Christian in English and Swahili as in Latin. But it may mean a great deal more to the worshiper if it is in his native tongue.

On the other hand, there are people who have changed

[13] Rembert Weakland, O.S.B., *Worship in a Secular World*, IDOC Papers, Rome (January 20, 1968), p. 6.

little. It would be the worst of mistakes to force them to change simply because others have. We have no right to yank the rug out from under those who are quite satisfied with the normal eleven o'clock Protestant service. The almost exclusively verbal forms of expression may be just right for those over thirty since these are the forms of expression and perception most congenial for them. If these forms are valid for those people, then the use of such forms must be continued. We have no right to force people to accept anything less valid for them. They have no need of new forms of worship. The usual eleven o'clock style of service ought to be continued as long as there are people who find it a satisfactory way of offering their worship to God.

But the converse is also true. These people need to be tolerant of those who find such forms of worship dull and meaningless. It is no longer realistic to say that everyone ought to worship in the way that seems natural to a forty-year-old middle-class white. To meet the needs of others, the church must provide alternate forms before those who are not middle aged and middle class vacate the church altogether. For many it is already too late. It is to help minister to these people for whom purely verbal forms are insufficient that this book is written. We do not mean for an instant that anything goes as long as it is relevant and currently modish. That is why we join to our pastoral norm theological and historical ones. But we do want to emphasize the need to start with people.

It is easier, after all, to change forms than people, so long as we abide within sound theological and historical norms. It should not surprise us that the possibilities before us are infinitely more varied than ever before in history since never before has human life been so complex and so rich.

Our pastoral norm, then, demands that we not only know people but that we accept them. Obviously we cannot as individuals accept and share with enthusiasm in all the forms of worship that a diverse society will need. But we do need to recognize the varieties of needs and to accept their legitimacy. Of course this means that the minister's work as leader of worship is likely to expand considerably in the future. Just as we have turned much of the educational work of the ministry on the large church staff over to a specialist—the director or religious education—so we may one day look for another specialist on such staffs—the liturgical director. He may not lead services himself (some have been laymen), but he will coordinate the numerous services of worship offered each week by differing groups within the congregation. And in some of these he may very well have a function not dissimilar to that of a producer in the theater.

In this aspect of ministry we are called upon to know people, to accept them, and to serve them. The pastoral norm for developing new forms of worship will test our adequacy at each of these steps—knowing, accepting, and serving.

II
WHAT IS CHRISTIAN WORSHIP?

We have seen the importance of knowing what is happening to people in order to understand how the forms of worship must be shaped and reshaped. But this is by no means enough by itself. New forms of worship must be evaluated in the light of the two other norms: theological and historical. Our present concern is within the first of these; the other follows in the next chapter.

It is perhaps indicative that we have begun with a discussion of people rather than with theology. A decade ago I wrote an article entitled "The God Whom We Worship." Now I have commenced with what could have been entitled "The People Who Worship." Many others have noticed a similar shift of attention. It is necessary, however, to keep both sides of the coin in mind. Talking about people is only one pole of our discussion. Christian worship involves consideration of God as well as of man. When we slight either, we are not talking about Christian worship any longer. To neglect sociology, as we once did, is just as misleading as overlooking theology, as sometimes seems to be the temptation for experimenters today.

We shall try in this chapter to delineate from a theological perspective the distinctive qualities of Christian worship. Often a great deal of effort and enthusiasm are spent on an experimental service of worship. Everyone feels exhilarated by the event and goes home speaking of what a great experience it has been. But the question remains, lurking deep down inside their consciousness: "Was it really Christian worship?"

This is a very important question even though often ignored by enthusiastic experimenters. Surprisingly many of these same people would disdain a revivalistic service as emotional exploitation, yet they judge their own services by their power to stir people. Christian worship is not to be judged solely by its ability to titillate the emotions any more than by its ability to intrigue the intellect. The catharsis of watching something as sublime as Aeschylus' *Agamemnon* or the emotional bath of viewing a sentimental movie are not to be confused with Christian worship. At the same time, a sermon is hardly adequate when the only difference between it and a lecture is the duration of thirty minutes. Certainly worship involves the intellect and the emotions. Otherwise the worshipers would be less than fully human. Christian worship does have a definite content which is difficult, if not impossible, to distinguish entirely from the forms that have conveyed that content. But we shall make the effort to analyze that content in this chapter and match it with the forms themselves in the next.

The content of many recent innovative services seem to many people vague and amorphous, the whole stress being placed on enthusiastic involvement. To be sure, the old distinctions between education and entertainment have often been erased today. But, McLuhan to the contrary, not all that entertains educates, and much that engrosses may also pervert. It is a chilling thought that the modern masters of pageantry were the Nazis. Not only were they extremely creative in their spectacles, but they also evoked a high degree of participation. The lesson ought to be clear; simply using Christian symbols as part of the *décor* does not baptize a bacchanal.

It is tempting in an age when we realize how closely the medium and the message are linked to leave all to the medium and to be indifferent to the message. This temptation makes it all the more crucial that we attempt to articulate the meaning of Christian worship before we try to express it in new forms. We need to be clear about the message itself before we seek new media for it. Experimentation which begins by taking a theological shortcut can be thrilling, but it may do more tearing down than building up of the community of faith.

We shall tackle two very difficult questions in this chapter: "What is Christian worship?" and "Why is it important to Christian life?" These inquiries ought to precede any experimentation in worship. The tentative answers we give here are meant only to provoke others to wrestle with these concerns. Until one has probed deeply in this area he has no more business trying out new forms of worship than he has taking unlabeled medicines. Essentially the theological norm is the investigation of any act of worship as to its adequacy in reflecting Christian faith.

I

There are few terms more difficult to define than "Christian worship." When one considers the variety of mentalities it has encompassed in the span of twenty centuries, the cultures it has changed and been changed by, and the present-day practice of Christian worship by congregations in all but five countries of the globe, it seems positively reckless to attempt a comprehensive definition. Though the risks are obvious, it is an undertaking we cannot avoid.

The definition we shall attempt is this: _Christian worship is the deliberate act of seeking to approach reality at its deepest level by becoming aware of God in and through Jesus Christ and by responding to this awareness._ Such a definition requires considerable explanation.

Worship involves a shift in gears as far as our normal consciousness is concerned. Much of life is like listening to a scratched record in which we constantly hear the record noise but only at intervals become aware of the beautiful music being played beneath the din. It is in intervals such as these that we penetrate beneath superficial reality and perceive things in terms of ultimate reality. In this sense, worship involves a discontinuity with the rest of our mental activities, few of which are devoted to examining things in the light of the presence of God. The deliberate probing in depth for reality that worship demands is not a flight from the world but a means of being with the world and oneself at a more profound level. Far from being otherworldly, it leads to deeper and fuller engagement with the world, now glimpsed as the arena of God's action. Genuine worldliness is possible only through the depth in which worship makes us encounter the world. It leads to treating the world with the full seriousness it deserves rather than simply with the top layer of our consciousness.

What does it mean to become aware of God? One can use other words and speak of worship as becoming conscious of, of recognizing, of perceiving the presence of God. Obviously God is no more present to the worshiper than the nonworshiper. But the worshiper becomes aware of God's presence. We can speak of worship as giving insight into things as they really are. One perceives the inner nature of things, rediscovering everything as dependent upon God.

Worship does not usually mean the imparting of new knowledge or the transmission of new information about God. It involves, rather, a rediscovery of the salvation events which we already know—and constantly forget. One can speak of this as reconsideration or recollection since it is a return to what we have known before. Reconsideration of past events brings anew the realization that God acts in our own midst. As we worship we rediscover what we once knew, professed, and forgot, that everything in the world depends upon God. It is no new insight but one that quickly vanishes from the mind until recovered in worship.

Recollection in Christian worship consists to a high degree in the commemoration of historic events that the Christian community remembers as clues to the meaning of all history. The life and death of Jesus Christ stand out above all else as the key disclosures of God acting in human history. The Christian believes that God is working in the present largely because of the community's memories of his past activity. It is for this reason that a major portion of almost any service of Christian worship is a rehearsal of the community of faith's corporate memories of God's acts as narrated in Scripture. The continued reconsideration of these past events in the worshiping community enables the worshiper to reappropriate for himself once again that on which his knowlege of God is based.[1]

[1] Cf. my *Worldliness of Worship* (New York: Oxford University Press, 1967), Chapters II and III for more detail on concepts outlined here.

In becoming aware of God we acquire insight, not only into the nature of God, but of our relation to the world itself, to our neighbor, and to ourselves. When world, neighbor, and self are seen *sub specie aeternitatis*, they emerge in true perspective. Through the act of reconsideration, the true nature of reality once again reveals itself. We rediscover among other things the world as created, God as present in one of the least of these our neighbors, and ourselves as both sinners and God's image. We knew all this already, but without the constant reiteration of worship such insight slips from our mind. These insights into reality are renewed through worship daily and weekly.

But worship does not stop there. This awareness of God which we rediscover demands a response almost inevitably. One responds because he has found insight that is valid and significant for his own life. Of course it is easy simply to mouth verbal responses, but the most adequate responses in worship are spontaneous acclamations of that which has been rediscovered. In this sense, response ought to be qualified by the word "fitting" since we respond to something prior with that which is "meet and right." Response, then, is a reciprocal action, concordant with the insight received. Declaration of man's sin leads to a response of confession; proclamation of God's works prompts a response of praise.

Such responses are both intensely corporate and personal. The group is one in its response, and yet the individual expresses the significance to him of what he has recollected. An important part of the personalizing of what is proclaimed in worship is the individual's own affirmation, ranging verbally anywhere from a faint "amen" to a shouted "hallelujah," in which he affirms the validity of these insights.

The basic character of response in Christian worship has been that of praise and thanksgiving. One rejoices and gives thanks to God for the evidence of his love of which we have been freshly made aware. Praise is based upon the prior love of God. "We love because he loved us first." We praise him because his love has again been disclosed to us in worship. Praise is the basic and inevitable response to rediscovery of the activity of God, to the fresh awareness "from whom all blessings flow." The psalms catch this often in their recital of what God has done for his people and his people's response. Frequently the essence of worship is summed up in a single psalm verse. The writer of Psalm 8 reflects: "When I look at thy heavens, the work of thy fingers," which leads him to exclaim: "How majestic is thy name in all the earth!"

There are, of couse, many other elements of response in worship. Western Christianity has probably overdone its stress on the element of contrition over man's sin. Too, one does rediscover himself as sinner in worship but, far more important, he discovers that Christ died for his sin. Confession is important, but far more important is the declaration of pardon. The offering of oneself in mission to others is an important response in worship. This arises from a reconsideration of God's having already given himself for us. Our awareness of dependence upon God leads to voicing of our needs (petition) and the needs of others (intercession). The basic sense in these and other responses is: this being so, I react to show its effect for my life.

Let us hope that our definition of Christian worship begins to make sense at this point. It was: Christian worship is the deliberate act of seeking to approach reality at its deepest level by becoming aware of God in and through Jesus Christ and by responding to this awareness.

In the present world, Christian worship encounters problems for every aspect of this definition. Since these challenges are the chief reason for this book's existence, let us look more closely at the difficulties facing Christian worship as defined above. We can follow our three-part division of depth, insight, and response as the easiest way of laying out the problems confronted.

Approaching reality at its deepest level is not easily done in the modern world when our minds are so constantly bombarded with information, most of it of transient nature and slight significance. The ephemeral and obvious are so omnipresent that the deeper significance and meaning of things get lost in the shuffle. It is not a question of "The world is too much with us" but rather that the outer shell, the appearances, of the world are "too much with us." We do not mean by worship a flight from the world but encounter with the world on a level of understanding. Worship is an attempt to answer the question: "Lord, when was it that we saw you?" by reminding ourselves of the real nature of that which is already about us.

But it is too easy to ignore this, to live on the top layer of our consciousness, never to penetrate beneath the surface. Anyone who has refinished antique furniture knows how he has to strip away layer after layer of paint before he can rediscover the beauty of the wood itself. But it is much easier to go on living on that top layer of consciousness, never to go beyond outward appearances. Certainly this is the way we glimpse many, if not most, of the people we know. We only see the image they are trying to project, we do not really know them.

In the modern world it is largely a question of time. Despite all our laborsaving devices we are busier than ever before. Cardinal Jean Daniélou, S.J., made a strong case for the need to recover time to devote to the contemplation of life in his book *Prayer as a Political Problem*. He challenges governments to seek ways of making life less frenetic so that "conditions in which prayer is possible" can be achieved.[2] For most men the pace of modern life allows very little time for probing life in depth. Bread and circuses, instead, occupy our waking hours.

Yet worship demands a break of pace, an opportunity to step aside from the main track for a few moments in order to see where we are going. The monastic builds his daily schedule around such a pattern but the rest of us have to fight an uphill battle to make it possible. So the first, and perhaps the greatest, problem is that of finding the time to disengage our minds from surface reality in order to approach life from depth so that we may reengage in the world in a deeper and more profound way. Certainly simply being in church does not guarantee that our minds are disengaged from superficiality. Distraction creeps in the church door just as it does anywhere else. Our mind is as cluttered when we come to worship as it is at any other time. Our worship has to compete with the other thoughts that crowd our mind. The interlude of Saturday does bring a certain release from the tensions

[2] (London: Burns & Oates, 1967), p. 40.

of the work week (except to mothers), and people may be even more relaxed on Sunday evening. And perhaps it takes more than one lonely hour to clear the static from our minds.

At any rate, we need to think through the necessity of what the Quakers call "centering down" or "finding one's inward center." Worship is highly influenced by the expectations with which people approach it. We need to help people come to worship with the sense that here they come to approach all of life in a greater sense of depth than our normal consciousness allows opportunity for.

Similar problems arise with the question of becoming aware of God. As we have discussed in chapter one, the forms of perception of modern man are changing drastically. The new electronic media with their ability to stimulate several of the senses have the power to involve man much more fully than an exclusively verbal medium. They demand fullness of participation. It is no wonder that the *Constitution on the Sacred Liturgy* speaks of "that full, conscious, and active participation in liturgical celebrations which is *demanded by the very nature of the liturgy.*" [3]

There is no reason why Christan worship should limit itself to certain forms of communications, if the times have contributed new and more effective media. What matters is not that specific forms be retained but that we use forms effective in making us aware and conscious of God, what he has done, does, and promises to do for us. The corporate memories of the church must be communicated to each generation, but the means by which the good news is proclaimed is not restricted only to those media which have proved successful in the past.

The question arises as to how explicit the Christian insight has to be. We have been accustomed in Protestantism to rehearsing our awareness of God through high definition media, that is, the message has been spelled out in explicit fashion, little being left for the imagination of the worshiper to add. [4] Low definition media, by contrast, demand a higher degree of participation in that the individual has to supply more of the content. In the past, what we have been asked to become

---

[3] *Documents of Vatican II*, p. 144. (Italics mine.)
[4] Cf. Marshall McLuhan, *Understanding Media*, p. 36.

aware of in worship has been largely, perhaps excessively, concretized in words. We were told, or read, or recited precisely what we believed, felt, or confessed. Words made it very clear.

Today many are experimenting in forms of worship that do not convey Christian insight verbally. A great deal more is left for the imagination of the worshiper to contribute. How explicitly must the contents of the Christian awareness of God be defined? This is not the same as asking how verbal worship must be to be Christain, since poetry is verbal and yet often highly ambiguous and undefined. But can a service in which, say, Scripture is not read or exegeted and central Christian symbols are never verbalized or visualized be deemed Christian worship? Does a slide show of the sufferings of the world, moving as it may be, qualify to be called Christian worship?

These are by no means easy questions to answer. In the first place, much that passes for Christian worship can be doctrinally correct and yet be so remote and detached from life that it neither conveys meaningful insight nor elicits sincere response. Certainly verbalization does not guarantee worship, no matter how orthodox the words. Secondly, Christian worship has always included nonverbal elements. Instrumental music is always an abstract form to which one contributes his own concepts. And instrumental music has been a prominent ingredient in Protestant worship. Even when we have been most insensitive to visual arts, the building has produced an environment which has affected us whether we were conscious of it or not. The Quakers, too, have long cherished forms of worship in which frequently no words are spoken. It is, then, a question of degree. How highly defined does the consciousness of God have to be? How explicit must we be? What are our expectations? Perhaps we can say that to qualify as Christian worship a service must be concordant with the corporate memories of the church as expressed in Scripture though not necessarily reproducing these memories in words. This would mean that the basic scriptural themes must be discoverable if not verbalized. It also excludes a great deal of verbalized material that occasionally poses as Christian worship—the poetical mysticism of Kahlil Gibran, for example.

Ultimately the touchstone of Christian worship must be its transparency to the communities' memories, the historic revelation transmitted to us through Scripture.

If these memories of meaning events are recovered, whatever the means, we can say that the raw material of Christian worship is provided. And if these events which the Christian community has found to be the source of its life together are not rehearsed in worship, whatever the means employed, then one cannot fairly label the service "Christian worship."

It seems increasingly apparent with the media we now have that there is less need to rely so exclusively on verbal symbols to communicate the awareness of God. If other forms of communication will serve the same purpose, especially if they will draw the worshiper into fuller interaction with Christian awareness, then we can rely less on words alone. This does not mean that verbal forms can be lightly dispensed with any more than this has happened in the rest of life which still depends heavily on verbal communication. But no longer must we be restricted to verbal forms of worship any more than in the rest of life. Our chief concern is that the insight communicated reflects the Christian community's understanding of God's action for his people and not just a reductionist doctrine of the fatherhood of God and the brotherhood of man, sublime though those concepts may be. Christian faith goes a good deal deeper in showing forth the source of genuine brotherhood through the love of God revealed in Jesus Christ.

Obviously, too, the variety of cultures and subcultures in the world will increasingly demand a variety of forms for representing the Christian consciousness of God. For many people, especially those of middle age, the present-day forms of Protestant worship will probably remain the best vehicle for communicating Christian insight about God. But other patterns will be indicated for children, youth, racial minorities, etc. In each case, the essential criterion of the forms would be the ability to show forth the corporate memories of the church as expressed in Scripture.

Other problems arise when we speak of worship as involving a response to the awareness of God. Response is essential since it gives us the opportunity to appropriate for ourselves the group's consciousness of God. One does not simply absorb insight like a sponge; one reacts with joy, sorrow, thankfulness, and sacrifice. But the forms we have used in the past to convey these responses have increasingly proved inadequate. For the most part such responses were verbal, ranging from a terse "amen" to a stylized dialogue. We were encouraged, in effect, to tell how we felt but only in a proper and decorous fashion.

That is the core of the problem; the forms of response of the recent past have been tied to a tight concept of good taste. The period of 1920 to 1970 has been the period of respectability for Protestant worship in this country. We got embarrassed out of the fervent "amen" during sermons or the exclamation of "hallelujah" at any point in the service. We got accustomed to letting choirs sing the responses, and docilely we read only the words printed for us in the bulletin. Anything spontaneous disappeared and the services became as smooth as butter. Nothing unexpected happened; there were no risks. When the service was broadcast or telecast it would end very promptly at 11:59:59.

All this may have been fine for those times. Most of the people in the churches of the major denominations had two goals in life: security and comfort. And our churches certainly echoed those virtues. Nothing unexpected ever happened, nothing ever rocked the boat, one could worship with full confidence in the stability of things as they were. And the engineers saw to it that we kept comfortable with cushioned pews, air conditioning, and indirect lighting. No burning bushes, mind you, just soft pleasant indirect lighting.

Few of us noticed that the fastest growing churches, here and abroad, tended to be of the Pentecostal variety with their emphasis on spontaneity in worship. The unexpected could and did happen; not just in occasional outbursts of glossolalia, but in frequent and fervent responses expressed in shouts and songs.

The situation today has changed throughout Christendom. Pentecostalism has had a tremendous appeal to the youth in, of all places, Catholic colleges. Much of society is now much less inhibited in the way it responds to all of life. Quietly mouthed responses seem hardly enough for a world that expects demonstrations, strikes, protests, or marches to be listed in the daily papers. Nor are we likely to find words alone enough in a world that bombards us with the visual, with movements, and with all kinds of sensory inputs. The forms of response of the immediate past seem too tame, too subdued, too restrained to reflect the tremendous significance for us of what we have rediscovered in worship.

We cannot simply duplicate in middle-class white congregations the cultural forms that work well for uneducated blacks or whites. But we can learn a great deal from their spontaneity, their high degree of participation, and their willingness to expect the unexpected. This can be a real liberation for those of us who have been accustomed to buttoned-down worship in which everything must proceed down the page in an orderly progression, in which we always have to go from beginning to end, and in which only one thing happens at a time. But it does not guarantee that the same musical, spoken, and other forms can easily be transplanted into the alien soil of the middle-class suburban congregation.

The problem is further complicated by the fact that such a wide variety of responses is evoked by Christian worship. Adoration gives way to contrition; contrition gives way to thanksgiving. At times the offering of money, our service, our prayer, and ourselves are indicated. Thus the forms expressive of these responses encompass the whole gamut of human emotions. There may be a few constants. The presence of music tends to heighten the intensity of whatever is said. Appropriate actions rather than words alone also underscore impact of the varied responses.

It seems likely that we shall move away from responses that are exclusively verbal to those that involve gestures, movements, sounds, and sights. Again the question arises as to how explicit such responses must be considered appropriate for Christian worship. Is a procession an adequate substitute for a creedal affirmation of faith? Can dance express with sufficient clearness our contrition after a call to confession?

A valid criterion may be that these forms of response must express in a profound way the reaction of the community to the insight gained in worship. Responses do not manifest directly the scriptural witness to God, conveyed in reconsideration, but they need to reflect the effect of such insight. This is a more diffuse and diverse area than the communication of insight itself since responses are obviously so dependent upon the individuals in the group. The insight reflects the church's awareness of its corporate memories. The responses reflect the individual's own reaction from being touched by rediscovery even as part of the community. Thus there would seem to be a greater area for expression, less insistence upon conformity, and considerably less pressure for responses that are explicitly articulated in traditional Christian terms. Obviously there are some limits when a response is likely to give offense to others. But in this area there ought to be considerable liberty for a greater variety of reactions occurring spontaneously and simultaneously. Some will dance and some will not; others may shout and some be silent. After all we lived with a degree of spontaneity in Protestant worship before we got so respectable. Some responded to an altar call and some remained seated; amens were spontaneous though not always unpredictable. We have a wider range of verbal and nonverbal responses open to us than did our grandfathers. We hope we will be free enough to use them in the worship of God.

II

Worship is apparently going to take more preparation and planning, in short, to make greater demands upon the time of minister and worship committee. Not only must the person responsible prepare a sermon, as in the past, but he must spend an increased amount of time securing or creating visual materials and other props, in coordinating the increased number of people who have special roles in the services, and in planning a greater variety of types of worship. In short, he will often play the role of a producer, whereas today his work has chiefly consisted in preparing a sermon and prayers and in choosing hymns, lessons, and prayers. Characteristically, these have been almost entirely word-centered activities. There is plenty of indication that planning and preparing for worship will take more rather than less of a minister's time in the future.

How can this be justified in a time when the ministers are already so busy? Still more, how can it even be considered in a world aflame with revolution? We are forced, at least, to question the importance of worship for the Christian life. Does worship merit the expenditure of as much time and talent as preparation for it now seems to demand? Our answer is "yes" because of conviction that worship is at the very center of the church's mission. Evangelism, social action, nurture, education, all grow out of worship like the petals from the center of a flower.

The times seem to make it increasingly evident how much man lives by symbols. In the early 1970s the role of the peace symbol and the American flag are good indications as to the power of symbols to evoke underlying realities in national life. The peace symbol itself, having evolved from a "ban the bomb" symbol in post-World-War-II Britain, became a generalized antiwar symbol by the 1970s. But its particular potency in 1970 was a specific reference to its identification with American withdrawal from the Vietnam War. As such, it came to have the power to provoke support and opposition, sometimes even to the point of violence.

The same pattern developed with the American flag which came to be increasingly identified with approval of American policies in Vietnam. Instead of being a generalized symbol of all Americans, it increasingly referred to a hawkish position with regard to Vietnam. Patriotic Americans found themselves not flying their flags because they did not wish flag flying to be interpreted as a symbol of blanket approval of American policies. The flag fliers became increasingly sanguine and made rigid laws against any disrespect to the flag. Ironically, many of the same people, when discussing the consecrated bread and wine in the Lord's Supper, would say it was "only a symbol." But when a person burnt the flag they somehow lost their sense of humor and put him in jail.

Man lives by and for his symbols. He must have something to make the intangible tangible, the invisible visible. A national debate necessitates symbols of the alternatives, perhaps a bit too polarized in the case of flag versus peace symbol. The same thing is true of the Christian life. We need ways to show forth the realities which the Christian understands as underlying life itself. Worship gives us the opportunity to symbolize the ultimate realities of life itself. The realities of life are not made to exist by worship any more than the flag makes America. But, like the flag, worship gives to these realities a focus, making them real by making them real to our perception of them. The love of God exists independently of our worship. But in worship we rediscover and respond to this love in such a way that it can change the rest of our lives.

We can speak, then, of worship as a mirror of reality. We see how things really are and respond to them. And yet our vision soon grows dim and we must worship again and again. In this sense, worship is essential to the Christian life because the conditions of human life demand a fresh symbolizing of reality. Take away all visual and verbal symbols of nationhood, and patriotism is likely to disappear. Take away Christian worship, and it is hard to conceive of Christianity as long enduring. It is only natural that Vatican II spoke of the liturgy as "the summit toward which the activity of the Church is directed; at the same time it is the fountain from which all her power flows." [5] Worship certainly does not eliminate other aspects of the Christian life but rather serves as their summit and source.

We need to push this further. Perhaps it is best done by examining two purposes the church has long seen fulfilled in worship. The church has regarded worship as functioning both for the glorification of God and for the sanctification of man. Obviously neither of these functions is isolated from the other but they do form two poles of emphasis in discussion of worship. How does worship work for the glorification, i.e., the praising of God? And how does worship work for the sanctification, i.e., the making holy or perfecting, of Christian man?

Worship acts as the summit and source of the Christian life by constantly revealing the "why" of Christian living. It is a constant reminder of what it's all about, a mirror of reality. In traditional terms, worship is a "means of grace," empowering and enabling one to be a disciple of Christ. John Wesley spoke of three such "means of grace," as sanctifying or perfecting the Christian life: "the way of prayer," "in searching the Scriptures," and "in partaking of the Lord's Supper." [6] Let

[5] "Constitution on the Sacred Liturgy," *Documents of Vatican II*, p. 142.
[6] "The Means of Grace," *Sermons on Several Occasions* (London: Epworth Press, 1956), pp. 139-44.

us look briefly at how these three means of grace operate for the sanctification of man. We shall not follow Wesley's exposition but attempt a contemporary statement.

Prayer is of many types—confession, praise, thanksgiving, petition, intercession—to name just a few. In all these we open ourselves to God and place our thoughts and desires before that which is ultimate. Prayer becomes our most frequent opportunity to articulate that which is deepest in our lives. It is also the occasion, especially in intercessory prayer, in which our concern for all mankind is widened. Our consciousness reaches out to a wider variety of mankind in prayer than we meet any day. As the church joins in prayer for "all sorts and conditions of men," we recall our concerns for the benefit of all men. Prayer is a call to "benevolence to being in general," to wishing and to working for the good of all men whom we rediscover as God's creatures too. If prayer changes things, it begins by changing the person who prays. It helps him see his creaturehood and responsibility to God and hence to his fellowman. In this way, the Christian life is shaped by prayer both in private devotions and in public worship. Prayer is the beginning of service to others.

The role of the Scriptures in the Christian life is also essential. They contain the corporate memories of the church and give to it self-identity. Without the Scriptures the church would simply be an amorphous conglomeration of people of good will without any identity. There is a parallel in the nation. We are Americans, though comprised of a wide variety of national origins, because we share common history. Even the newly naturalized American appropriates as his own the historical experiences of colonization, revolution, westward migration, civil war, and emergence as a world power. Naturalization ceremonies often dwell upon the new citizen's appropriation of this history. Through the reading and exposition of Scripture, the Christian recovers for himself the experiences of Israel and the early church: escape from slavery, conquest, captivity, hope for a messiah, incarnation, crucifixion, resurrection, and mission.

The church in worship regularly recovers not just these events but the meaning that it has discovered in them. They become God events though they happen in the midst of secular history.

But in the events narrated in Scripture the Christian community discerns meaning that illumines all history. Suddenly the black and white of history has been transformed into a color presentation. A major part of Christian worship is the rehearsal of these meaning-events which give us clues for interpreting life in the present and future as well as in the past as involving God's actions.

In similar fashion, the Lord's Supper, and baptism too, convey to us the reality of God's actions for us. We certainly do not intend a full discussion of the sacraments at this point. Protestantism has been excessively stringent in demanding explicit biblical warrants for the sacraments though retaining other acts without the name of the sacrament. We shall mention here only the Lord's Supper and baptism.

There are many aspects to baptism mentioned in the New Testament. Such metaphors as union to Christ, incorporation into the church, the new birth, forgiveness of sin, and reception of the Holy Spirit are the most obvious.[7] But what concerns us here is the sense of baptism as a way of life. Every time the Christian community gathers for worship and a child of God (of whatever age) is baptized, the love of God in accepting us as we are is shown forth. We do not baptize; we are baptized. Here God acts to show us his love in uniting us to the community of faith, to those who are being saved. Something happens in baptism; God through his church makes us members of Christ's body on earth. The consequence is that every time we take part in baptism, God's prevenient love in accepting us is shown forth. Luther could exclaim that "there is no greater comfort on earth than baptism."[8] He exulted that "I am baptized" and "God, who cannot lie, has bound himself in a covenant with me."[9] Baptism, then, is part of a Christian style of life, for it is a constant reminder of what God has done for us, conveyed to us in a most personal and intimate way. In baptism my name was spoken, my head (or

---

[7] Cf. my *Worldliness of Worship*, pp. 132-45.
[8] "The Holy and Blessed Sacrament of Baptism," *Luther's Works* (Philadelphia: Muhlenberg Press, 1960), XXXV: 34.
[9] *Ibid.*, p. 36,

body) was washed. I have taken the surname of the Trinity, I was baptized into the family of God, and every time I witness the baptism of another, God's promises are renewed to me also.

Augustine somewhere makes a comment that the Lord's Supper is the only part of baptism that is repeated. In his time baptism, confirmation, and first communion occurred together. But it is true in a more profound sense. Every time we share in the Lord's Supper, God's love is again shown forth to the gathered Christian community. Of course the method is different. In the Lord's Supper, Christ gives himself for us again just as he once gave his body for us on the cross. But this is a gift that only the eye of thanksgiving can discern. The biblical metaphors for the Lord's Supper are varied, but each one adds a new facet. They suggest thanksgiving, communion fellowship, the commemoration of Christ's work, the memorial of his sacrifice, and the presence of Christ.[10] All these dimensions must be kept in mind to have a balanced concept of this sacrament. In modern terms, we might say that the Lord's Supper is an act in which Christ again gives himself to us enabling us to give ourselves for others.

We have tried to show how in these three ways—through openness to God in prayer, through the study and exposition of the church's memories of God's acts, and through his actions in the sacraments—the Christian is enabled to live a Christian life. But what about the other pole of worship, the glorification of God? Recent tendencies could be interpreted as overshadowing this dimension. In the Vatican II *Constitution on the Sacred Liturgy* the sanctification of man is mentioned before the glorification of God in over twenty instances.[11]

Yet in a narrow sense, much of worship does revolve around the glorification of God. One rarely rehearses the memories of the church without glorifying God for what he has done. Psalms and hymns are interspersed with the lessons. Almost inevitably the recital of God's benefits produces responses of praise and thanksgiving. The same holds true of the sacraments

[10] Yngve Brilioth, *Eucharistic Faith and Practice, Evangelical and Catholic* (London: S.P.C.K., 1953).

[11] Godfrey Diekmann, O.S.B., *Personal Prayer and the Liturgy* (London: Geoffrey Chapman, 1969), p. 57.

—55—

and prayer. The normal response to a gift is gratitude to the giver. And, of course, the glorification of God is a part of the sanctification of the believer, for it is a constant direction of his thoughts and attention to that which is ultimately real in life.

In a wider sense, the sanctification of man is the glorification of God. As man through worship moves to a greater concern about his life before God and among men, he tries to reflect the love of God in concern for his neighbor. Out of thanksgiving to God, he acts for man. We can speak of the result of worship being doxological living, i.e., living for others because of gratitude for God's gifts. In this sense, all life is lived for the glorification of God. The glorification of God is brought about outside worship as well as within it. Our praise of God does not end with the final "amen" of the service; it has only begun at that point.

Ultimately, of course, sanctification and glorification of God are one. Worship builds us up to live effective Christian lives of concern for all of God's creatures. And in both worship and the rest of life we are both sanctified and glorifying God. Worship is an essential part of the Christian life and is well worth every effort it takes to make it meaningful for modern man.

III

HARD-CORE CHRISTIAN WORSHIP

Some of the most important experimentation in Christian worship occurred in the first, fourth, and sixteenth centuries. But there was also much innovative worship in the sixth, eighth, thirteenth, and nineteenth centuries. To be brief, new forms of worship have appeared in every century as peoples and cultures changed. All twenty centuries of the Christian era have been centuries of experimentation in worship. Twentieth-century liturgical experimentation must be seen in this context as the continuation of a well-established pattern of change rather than as the beginning of it.

Of course today we may be more conscious and deliberate about experimentation in worship. It is unlikely that previous eras were as self-conscious about everything they did and none had such a passion for statistics about everything from market research to sexual mores. The experiments of the past were rarely considered as such. They began simply as a solution for a local situation and need, but some ended up by spreading throughout the universal church. An architectural form devised as a convenience to monks, the divided chancel, was adopted by parish churches all over medieval Europe. We have, or at least assume we have, an advantage in a more conscious and deliberate approach, though future generations may think differently. At least we must realize that there is nothing new about experimentation in Christian worship but that we are simply adding the latest chapter to a long history of innovations.

Unfortunately, the average Protestant pastor is innocent of

much knowledge of the history of liturgical experimentation. Most Protestant seminary graduates have studied even less of liturgiology (the history of liturgy) than they have of sacramental theology. And few have felt particularly deprived since it never was brought to their attention that liturgiology ought to have been in their seminary curriculum. All too often the history of the church is not taught as a liberating discipline and even less often is it learned as such. Our basic thesis in this chapter is that a knowledge of the history of Christian worship is a necessary ingredient for significant experimentation in twentieth-century worship.

Santayana is usually credited with the saying that those who do not know history are forced to repeat it. This is certainly true with liturgical experimentation. A recently published text for an "experimental" eucharist turns out to be late medieval in all its emphases, contemporary only in its language. A little historical knowledge would have persuaded the compiler that the individualistic and penitential aspects of the eucharist hardly need underscoring in the twentieth century, whether in modern language or any other. There have been a lot of shipwrecks in the history of worship and there is no need to hit the same shoals again when liturgical scholarship has charted them well. The church building in the round was tried in the sixteenth century and rejected. Today, some millions of dollars later, we find that the sixteenth century was right. A circular building is far from ideal for both preaching and the sacraments.

The positive reason for the study of liturgiology is even stronger than that of avoidance of certain pitfalls. Such study gives us perspective on ourselves so we can see what needs to be done in our own time. It can teach us how changes in liturgy reflect social and cultural shifts and thus help us develop a sensitivity "to serve the present age." Liturgiology also calls to our attention situations in the past whose worship forms might serve parallel conditions in our own time.

Many of the most interesting experiments in recent times have been inspired by a return to practices common in the early church. When the early Christians celebrated the Lord's Supper, never knowing when a military patrol might break down the doors, they did not waste time on unessentials, any more than their successors today can afford to when they may be arrested for saying mass in front of the Pentagon or for using a church building as sanctuary for A.W.O.L. GI's. No single document has done so much to guide twentieth-century experimentation as a third-century document. *The Apostolic Tradition* of Hippolytus.[1] Hippolytus, a conservative Roman priest, has promoted modern liturgical experimentation by doing his very best to discourage it in ancient times. He wrote, at the beginning of the third century, to give apostolic sanction to the practices he was familiar with in Rome in the late second century. Hippolytus gives us valuable information on the early rites of the Lord's Supper, Christian initiation, ordination, private prayers, and the agape.

Marshall McLuhan insists that modern man is postliterate, that is, he has gone beyond dependence on the medium of the printed page as his prime means for communicating information after five hundred years of the Gutenberg age. In this, modern man has acquired perceptual patterns resembling, in some ways, those of preliterate man.[2] Both are heavily stimulated by the visual, by action, by the sense of touch to a greater degree than literate man (of whom there are a lot of us still around!). A renewed stress on nonverbal forms, characteristic of early and medieval Christian worship, once again makes sense to man. Protestantism turned its back on most such forms in the sixteenth century in favor of the then more modern forms of communication, especially the read word. Now it may be possible to move ahead by a long step backward, recovering from the early and medieval church practices that again communicate well to modern man.

Accordingly, our third norm for responsible experimentation in worship is that it be historically informed. This does not mean in the least that it be antiquarian or precious, though there are times and situations (as in a seminary chapel) when historic liturgies may be used both as a learning experience and

---

[1] The best edition is *La Tradition Apostolique de Saint Hippolyte* by Bernard Botte, O.S.B. (Muenster, Westfalen: Aschendorffsche Verlagsbuchhandlung, 1963). In English, Gregory Dix's translation, *The Apostolic Tradition of St Hippolytus of Rome,* has been reprinted (London: S.P.C.K., 1968). Cf. also Burton Scott Easton's edition, *The Apostolic Tradition of Hippolytus* (Hamden, Conn.: Archon Books, 1962).

[2] *Counterblast* (New York: Harcourt Brace & World, 1969), pp. 18, 36.

as a genuine worship of God. There are certain givens in Christian worship that may best be discovered by a study of the history of worship, indeed may only be discovered by this type of study. And we affirm that such study is of vital significance for stimulating and guiding the contemporary process of experimentation. We hope to indicate what these givens are in this chapter though space permits only a bare outline, a wave of the hand as we pass by.

We are convinced that experimentation in worship in ignorance of these givens of Christian worship is just as risky as trying to expound Christian doctrine without a knowledge of the Scriptures. It may be more sporting that way, but the score is not apt to be high. The result is all too often sentimentality and triviality no matter how much fun it all was. Entertainment is not the only function of Christian worship. A knowledge of history, to be sure, will not insure that a service is meaningful at a deep level, but when coupled with the pastoral norm and the theological norm it provides the best possible insurance.

The historical norm, then, operates by checking out our ideas by what the church has tried, retained, or discarded, and by asking "why?" in each instance. The study of history can make us more sensitive to the situations that dictate change and hence make us more willing to experiment. But by knowing what has been done and by asking "why?" we shall learn better how to serve our own times. The historical norm helps us clarify our intentions by cross-checking them with a vast file of experimentations over twenty centuries and six continents.

Though we may sound most conservative in insisting on the need for familiarity with the given of Christian worship, it has been our experience that the most radical experiments usually come from those who have the security of a solid historical background. The average Protestant minister is not quite sure which direction home is, so he timidly never strays too far. The Roman Catholic priest, on the other hand, has a certain security, knowing that he can always go home, hence he is willing to range further afield. Historical knowledge, as we have said before, is a liberating discipline since it gives us the confidence to be more radical. The *Underground Mass Book* [3] is a good example of a book wide-ranging in scope and beautifully relevant yet historically well-informed. It makes many Protestant efforts to do the same look neither particularly contemporary nor very adventuresome.

We have spoken of the "given" in Christian worship, and to this we now turn our attention. By the given we mean those forms that have everywhere and at all times been central in Christian worship. Scripture provides the given of Christian doctrine without by any means filling out the whole extent of Christian doctrine. Indeed, we are convinced we can speak of a "canon" of Christian worship just as definitely as we can of Scripture.[4] By the canon of Scripture we mean those books that by the end of the fourth century had come to be regarded as authoritative generally throughout the church. Four Gospels were chosen as canonical and all others excluded. A fourfold canon of worship becomes apparent by the end of the fourth century. Dr. Shepherd dates this a bit later (sixth century), but the essential ingredients had been worked out by the end of the fourth century and much appears as early as the New Testament period.

<u>The canon of Christian worship consists of four elements: the observance of time, the rites of initiation, the eucharist, and the divine office.</u> These four constitute hard-core Christian worship. There are of course many other forms of worship: the rites of passage (marriage, ordination, funerals), rites of reconciliation (penance, feasts, and fasts), sacred concerts, prayer meetings, revivals, and so forth. Some of these have long histories (ordinations), others relatively short ones (revivals); some have undergone a minimum of change (weddings), others reflect major changes (penance). They are not constants and may have been dispensed with or ignored altogether by massive segments of Christianity (anointing of the sick). Hence we do not consider them a part of hard-core Christian worship, important though they are. The canon, or hard core, as we prefer to call it, seems to be neglected only by a minority of small groups.

[3] Stephen W. McNierney, ed. (Baltimore: Helicon Press, 1968).
[4] Cf. Massey H. Shepherd, *Worship in Scripture and Tradition* (New York: Oxford University Press, 1963), p. 163.

The *Constitution on the Sacred Liturgy* of Vatican II mentions the permanent and the changing in worship: "for the liturgy is made up of unchangeable elements divinely instituted, and elements subject to change." [5] Though we may not want to attribute our canon of worship to divine authorship, the distinction between changeable and unchangeable is intriguing for anyone concerned about experimentation. Some things change and ought to change; others have a durability that ought not be overlooked. In this sense there is a real continuity in Christian worship analogous to the continuity that Scripture provides for theology.

This continuity is no mask for uniformity. Indeed, the more one studies history, the more amazing becomes the variety of ways the permanent elements can present themselves. As peoples and cultures have changed, so have the forms of these permanent elements been altered. Yet the more these permanent elements change, the more they seem to remain the same. They apparently possess an infinite flexibility. On the other hand, attempts to escape the permanent elements have been repeatedly tried, producing only small (though highly interesting) sects—Quakers, Shakers, Transcendentalists, etc.

We are not saying that these elements are adequate simply because they are old. But we can hardly afford to ignore those things which have proven valid "at all times, and in all places." A certain adequacy must be presumed, a certain closeness to essential human needs, a reflection of that which is changeless in man himself.

These hard-core elements cross the whole range of media, demanding the participation of all the physical senses as well as the sense of time. In the eucharist, baptism, and the divine office, one gets smell, taste, touch, sight, and hearing repeatedly involved in different ways.

Likewise, this canon of worship reflects an experience much wider than that of Christianity. Even though precise meaning comes from the Christian understanding of revelation, the whole canon reflects Jewish practices and mentality. Though we will not reiterate this, Jewish precedents and assumptions underlie the whole canon of worship called "Christian." We

[5] *Documents of Vatican II*, p. 146.

now look in turn at each of the four elements of hard-core Christian worship.

I

Ever since the first century, Christianity has used time as a means of communication. The whole structure of Christian worship is organized around the understanding that time is an important vehicle in communicating meaning. In *The Silent Language,* Edward T. Hall, an anthropologist, has traced various ways in which each of us uses time to communicate.[6] Being late in keeping an appointment makes a point that is often not missed, and anxiety to end the appointment is even more obvious. The way we use time is a subtle but vital communicator.

The chief function of time in Christian worship has been as a means of recovering key events in the history of revelation. A basic assumption in Christian worship is that God has disclosed himself to man in past events occurring in the midst of history. Worship becomes a way of regaining the significance of those past events for our present life. The ability to discover God in events comes into Christianity from Judaism. Though many of the Jewish feasts were nomadic or agricultural in origin, they soon became historicized. The Passover came to be a yearly renewal of the experience of deliverance from slavery in Egypt. When it was reenacted, it was as if the whole nation was reexperiencing what their forefathers lived through. And various cultic forms keep the significance of the original event alive throughout history right down to the present day.

The same possibility was glimpsed in the mystery religions of the Roman Empire in the first century. Various mythic events were celebrated in which the adherents of the sect reexperienced the crucial event in their god's life. Study of these cults gave Dom Odo Casel, O.S.B. (1886-1948) a deeper grasp of Christian worship. As Casel developed his mystery theology, he came to understand Christianity as celebrating the "primaeval saving act which is made present." [7] The original historical saving event of the life of Jesus is made present to

---

[6] (Garden City, N. Y.: Doubleday & Co., 1959), pp. 23-41.
[7] *The Mystery of Christian Worship* (Westminster, Md.: Newman Press, 1962), p. 124.

us in and through our acts of worship commemorating the event. In this commemoration, "Christ himself is present and acts through the church, his *ecclesia,* while she acts with him." [8] The original event is not repeated—that would make it meaningless. But its saving power, its significance to our lives, is recovered and given us to appropriate for ourselves. In this sense Casel speak of our living "our own sacred history." [9] Through representing the original event, we internalize it. It becomes part of our being, just as our national self-consciousness is shaped by celebrating the Fourth of July each year.

In the commemoration of the key events in salvation history, the meaning for our lives of these events is communicated. We know all year that Christ died for our sin, but on Good Friday this fact is brought home most dramatically. Time itself becomes a way of escaping the limitations of time. Thus the daily, weekly, and annual cycles of time become vehicles for bridging history and giving meaning to present life from past events.

For the Christian, the events recovered center in the life and ministry of Jesus Christ, even though the Christian week and two of the chief Christian festivals are built on Jewish foundations. The Christian year focuses on the birth and baptism of Jesus and the final events of his earthly ministry. The Marian feasts (Annunciation, Visitation, Presentation) have significance only as they point to Christ. Increasingly the explicitly doctrinal feasts (Trinity Sunday) and anatomical feasts (Precious Blood, Sacred Heart) have receded from importance. The feasts of the saints commemorate Christ's work after the descent of the Holy Spirit at Pentecost and serve to remind us of Christ's work through his Spirit in all times. Even All Saints' Day is really a christological feast, since it is Christ's work in his people that is celebrated.

The various cycles of time communicate by providing a variety of hymns, lessons, psalms, and prayers appropriate to each christological event. These elements that change according to the time cycles are known as "propers." The whole structure of Christian worship depends upon the various cycles of time in which the propers change according to the time of

[8] *Ibid.,* p. 141.
[9] *Ibid.,* p. 124.

day, the day of the week, or the day of the year. One does not
sing Christmas carols at Easter nor read the passion narratives
at Pentecost. Thus the propers give an immense variety to
Christian worship. Without the propers, Christian worship
would become completely routine and monotonous. Awareness
of the function of propers leads to a more lively presentation
of the fullness of the gospel. Children, our best teachers about
worship, have long demonstrated the importance of special occasions in communicating civic or historical meaning. A child
lives from Hallowe'en to Thanksgiving till Christmas, and so
on throughout the year. And much of what he learns about
America and Christianity is communicated by the yearly cycle
of time. The Christian year provides one of our best means for
adding interest and variety to worship.

Time has been organized in various structures by the church
in order to communicate the recalling of Christ. It should be
emphasized that these structures are far from neat and systematic, but this does not render them any less vital. Recent
attempts to tidy up the calendar by dividing the long season
after Pentecost have not been very successful, to say the least.
Let us quickly review the structures of time by which the
church helps us relieve the Christ event.

For most Christians, the structure of the day has no particular christological significance. There is evidence in the Old
Testament of private devotions as frequently as seven times
per day (Psalm 119:164) or thrice daily (Daniel 6:10). Early in
the second century A.D., the Didache recommended the
Christians say the Lord's Prayer "three times a day." By the
third century, Hippolytus was advising Christians to pray seven
times per day. Several of these "hours" were commemorative
of the crucifixion: Christ nailed to the cross at the third hour,
darkness at noon, and his shedding blood and water at the
ninth hour.[10] At midnight, Hippolytus tells us, "every creature
hushes for a brief moment to praise the Lord." [11] Eventual
monastic communities worked out a daily cycle of eight occasions of prayer (the "hours"), the whole comprising the divine
office.

[10] Gregory Dix, ed., The Apostolic Tradition of St Hippolytus of Rome,
pp. 62-64.
[11] Ibid., p. 67.

The origin of the Christian week again derives from the Jewish seven-day week, probably originally based on a Babylonian taboo of seven. The church very early, possibly within the lifetime of Paul, saw the first day of the week as a commemoration of the resurrection (Acts 20:7 ff.; Revelation 1: 10). This sense has remained throughout history; each Sunday is a little Easter, a remembrance of the resurrection. In time, Wednesdays and Fridays came to be observed as fast days, and Saturday was often tied to the honor of Mary.

At a very early time, the church began to use certain days of the yearly cycle as centers of meaning. The earliest of these, no doubt, was Easter, an annual as well as a weekly event. It took the place of the Jewish Passover as Pentecost did that of the Feast of Weeks. A third early feast, that of Epiphany (January 6), originally commemorated the birth and baptism of Jesus and came to signify the visit of the Magi in western Christianity. These were the earliest and the greatest of the feasts.

In the fourth century, Christmas displaced Epiphany as the commemoration of the nativity. Easter was split from Good Friday, the one representing the crucifixion, the other the resurrection. Ascension Day was separated from Pentecost, the first recalling the departure of Christ's physical body, the second the coming of his Spirit. Other festivals eventually appeared: Circumcision, Presentation in the Temple, Annunciation, Palm Sunday, Maundy Thursday, Visitation, Transfiguration to name the most important. In time, martyrs and other heroes of the faith were remembered, in most cases on the anniversary of their heavenly birthday (death). The Spirit of Christ had been recognized as working in them, so they represent a continuation of God's saving acts. At first they were recognized locally, then some of them gained worldwide recognition. To complicate matters further, there developed two annual cycles. One of these, the so-called sanctoral cycle, is made up of fixed days such as January 25 (Conversion of St. Paul) and November 1 (All Saints'). The temporal cycle includes those dates dependent on the date of Easter (Ash Wednesday, Pentecost) or on the dates of Sundays (Sundays of Advent) plus Christmas, Circumcision, and Epiphany. In effect, the church has two yearly cycles of time.

In some cases, it was obvious that a single day was not enough to commemorate an important event. Very early the fifty days from Easter to Pentecost were kept as the great fifty days during which, Tertullian tells us, no one fasted or knelt in worship.[12] Much later the final preparation of the catechumens for baptism at Easter was turned into a penitential season (Lent) duplicated by another before Christmas (Advent). The rest of the Sundays were numbered after Christmas, Epiphany, and Pentecost (or Trinity Sunday in northern Europe). For a few great feasts (finally only Christmas, Easter, and Pentecost) an octave (eight days) was observed, beginning on the eve before these feasts. In this way, all days of the year came to have a particular locus in salvation history. The intensity of this is much greater from December into May, with something of an off-season in January and the summer and fall months. The structures of time are ways of calling to mind one aspect after another of the work of God in Christ.

II

Ever since the birth of the church, Christianity has marked the beginning of people's allegiance to the church by rites of initiation. Indeed the Day of Pentecost included an occasion of mass baptism (Acts 2:41). Christian initiation includes such actions as baptism, confirmation, and first communion. Together these three acts form a major element of Christian worship.

The most obvious thing about Christian initiation is its temporal character. Not only does it mark a beginning, but it is also an ending. The exorcisms and the renunciation of Satan, a part of baptism since early times, mark a turning of one's back on the past just as much as other parts of the rite look to one's future. Initiation, then, has a very important temporal character. It draws a line between one's past life and his future life as a publicly avowed Christian. It makes a distinction between before and after in one's life through a public act.

Initiation as a Christian is a decisive act whether done for oneself or on the behalf of another. It is therefore natural that

[12] "De Corona," *Ante-Nicene Fathers* (New York: Scribners, 1899), III: 94.

initiation should be seen as imparting a permanent character. Just as a slave or soldier might be branded in the first century and bear the marks of servitude for life, so the sense remains that the new Christian becomes a marked man for life. It seems reasonable that the three traditional acts of initiation: baptism, confirmation, and first communion, come together. Instead, much of western Christianity has splintered initiation into three different occasions. As a decisive once-for-all act, it seems more appropriate for initiation to be completed at one time as with eastern Christians or as with adult converts' and believers' baptism in the West.

Initiation, beginning with baptism, is just the first of the rites of passage a Christian encounters. Marriage rites have been consolidated into a single ceremony (though often two sacraments—matrimony and eucharist—for many Christians) plus the reading of the banns previously in some Protestant and Catholic churches. Embarkation on church vocations is often marked by a commissioning office or ordination, sometimes in a series. Once again, the entrance on a new style of life is marked by worship. And death is marked by funeral rites.

Implicit, or even explicit is initiation in all these future rites. The union of man and wife is paralleled in one's union to the family of God in baptism, the naming of one's Christian name, and the contractual sense of the covenant relationship entered. It has become fashionable to speak of baptism as the ordination of the laity, though the laying on of hands (confirmation) is a closer ceremony to ordination. From Paul onward, the sense of baptism as death and resurrection has been explicit (Roman 6:3; Colossians 2:12) and is mimed in the act of submersion and rising.

The decisive character of Christian initiation is marked primarily by acts rather than words. Words play an important, though secondary, role in each stage of initiation. We signify decisive moments in life by actions rather than by words. Col. William Travis drew a line on the ground with his sword at the Alamo and those who intended to stay and sacrifice their lives stepped across. In the Roman Catholic Church at the ordination of subdeacons, the stage at which celibacy becomes mandatory, those who make this decision are told: "If you decide to persevere in your holy resolve, come forward." Actions speak louder than words at crucial moments.

Baptism, confirmation, and first communion demand acts and the use of matter. Something is done with water, bread, wine, and perhaps oil. Throughout the centuries the church has used these objects in highlighting the biblical metaphors associated with these rites. Union to Christ in his burial *(syntaphentes)* has long been dramatized by descent into the font and rising on the other side. Ancient baptistries utilized the same archiectural form as a mausoleum.[13] Baptism also joins us to Christ's church, best climaxed in sharing in his Supper with his people at the altar-table. Historically fonts were located near the entrance to churches because, in the Roman Catholic rite, one actually enters the church building in the course of the rite just as he actually enters the church in baptism. Baptism since New Testament times has been referred to as a new birth (John 3:5) or as regeneration (Titus 3:5), and this has been shown forth in the design of fonts that suggest a pregnant woman or the prayers for the blessing of the water that are as explicitly sexual as Christian worship ever gets. (At Easter Eve, the paschal candle dripped wax into the font, the candle was plunged in, and prayer offered that all those born of water might be begotten by grace.) Placing the past behind and the putting on of Christ was dramatized by putting a new white garment on the newly baptized. Forgiveness of sin is obvious in the washing, the fundamental act of baptism itself (cf. Acts 22:16). Reception of the Holy Spirit (John 3:5; Acts 2:38) and illumination have been reflected in the dove symbol and the act of giving a lighted candle to the newly baptized person.

The threefold structure of Christian initiation is recognizable among almost all those groups that practice the baptism of infants and children and frequently discernible in the groups that baptize only adult believers. Act one is that of washing with water, referred to as baptism.

There is less unanimity about the second act. The churches of the east have insisted on anointing as essential here, and certainly it has evidence in the biblical references to the anoint-

[13] Cf. J. G. Davies, *The Architectural Setting of Baptism* (London: Barrie & Rockliff, 1962), pp. 14-17.

ing or seal of the Spirit (II Corinthians 1:21-22; Ephesians 1: 13; 4:30). Roman Catholics continue this act. The Anglican communion dropped it in 1552, preferring to stress the laying on of hands. It is dubious if anointing with oil communicates anything to modern western man. In an age of kings or when the connection of the words chrism, Christ, and Messiah was obvious, anointing must have been a powerful symbolic act.

The churches of the West tended to make more of the act of laying on of hands, a biblical symbolic act connected with bestowal of the Holy Spirit (Acts 8:19; 19:6). Unfortunately, confirmation as a separate sacrament became a practice looking for a theology, but when seen as an integral part of baptism it makes good sense as a sign of the gifts of the Holy Spirit granted to those baptized into the family of God. Ironically, we are more accustomed to lay hands on the Bible in civil ceremonies than on people. But there is no more warm and human symbol of giving a person what one has received (the faith) than by the laying on of hands.

Most Protestants neglect the sense of first communion as the long-awaited admission to the Lord's table. He who has been joined to Christ is now welcome as guest at his table together with the Lord's own people. One feels adopted into a human family when he begins to eat with them, and the first such meal may be a great occasion. At first communion one joins the family of God gathered about his table. It is a fitting climax to Christian initiation and symbolic of its completion. He who once was outside the doors is now a sharer in holy things.

Obviously, our preference is that the three acts of Christian initiation belong together, though in the West they have become separated by a long series of factors extraneous to worship. It may not be so important as we have made it at what age initiation occurs, whether through the sponsorship of someone else who engages to bring us to faith or consciously and deliberately by ourselves when of age to understand. In either case, Christian initiation is a unity, and the three acts belong together. Ever after through our life they are renewed until the last rites. Penance or confession recapture the cleansing from sin, and communion and preaching nourish and renew the life lived in the covenant community. The important thing is that initiation marks the beginning of our life in Christ.

III

Our third element passes under a variety of names, a good indication of its complexity. The breaking of bread, divine liturgy, eucharist, mass, holy communion, Lord's Supper, and the Lord's Memorial are among the most important and give an indication of the variety of media we are dealing with here. It is not by accident that the Lord's Supper is both the heart of Christian worship and uses so many forms of communication.

Like most Christian worship, it is a time mystery. The Lord's Supper is most obviously a commemorative meal, recalling through both word and deed the events of the last supper, the passion, death, and resurrection as well as other events of salvation history. But it is equally a showing forth of the presence of the same Jesus Christ in our here and now. We use present tense for "this is . . ." in Greek, Latin, or English. But there is also a third time dimension, the meal anticipates a banquet in the future "when it finds its fulfillment in the kingdom of God." Time is a vehicle of communication in the Lord's Supper.

The Lord's Supper stimulates all the physical senses too. It is basically a sacred meal and involves all the sensory input that eating involves: seeing, touching, smelling, and tasting of food. Of course, we have made it such a stylized meal that we have forgotten that it represents a full meal with a cup of wine "after supper." We speak of the "Lord's table" or, at one time, of "God's board," but it is all too easy for us to forget we are taking part in the most common human social act, a meal together.

Physical action is a major part of this form of worship. As we shall see, the whole second half of the service is structured around actions. The New Testament name, the "breaking of bread" (Acts 2:42, 46; 20:7; I Corinthians 10:16), describes an action. Many find that the physical act of getting out of their pew and going forward to receive the bread and wine is one of the most meaningful parts of the service, though hard to define in words.

Of course words are spoken and sung so that hearing and speaking provide further levels of involvement in this form of worship. Indeed, a major emphasis is placed on narration and dialogue right at the very heart of the prayer of thanksgiving.

The centrality of the Lord's Supper in Christian worship since the first century is largely due to its ability to involve the worshiper totally, calling to attention all his senses as he joins in this form of worship. Each time, the Lord's Supper plunges right to the heart of the gospel. The very center of salvation history is shown forth, and it communicates in an instantaneous fashion the passion, death, and resurrection.

Despite the varieties of eucharistic rites which have been used, the most remarkable thing about the structure of these rites is their consistency. Nowhere else is the hard core of Christian worship more apparent than in the durability of the contents of the Lord's Supper. Under the most diverse circumstances, Christians have agreed that certain elements were central and permanent. We shall categorize these as four basic areas of consensus. It will be noted that many of these elements are apparent in Justin Martyr's description of the Lord's Supper in his "First Apology" dating from about A.D. 155.[14] and more fully in Hippolytus' model liturgy from the early second century, our earliest text for a eucharistic rite.[15] These areas of consensus appear from the beginning of known eucharistic rites and endure to the present.

The first consensus has been about the two-part nature of the Lord's Supper. From an early time, it became the custom to combine both the service of the Word, deriving from synagogue worship, with the service of the table, the upper-room ceremony. As Justin Martyr indicates, this two-part shape was already obvious by the second century.

There is a basic duality in the Lord's Supper deriving from the joining of two quite different forms and situations of worship, a public gathering and a private group. We show this in using the pulpit as the center of the first half and then moving to the altar-table for the second. Essentially two quite different dominant media have been brought together—the spoken

---

[14] Cf. Cyril C. Richardson, ed., *Early Christian Fathers* (Philadelphia: Westminster Press, 1953), pp. 285-87.

[15] Cf. Dix, ed., *The Apostolic Tradition of St Hippolytus of Rome*, pp. 6-9, 40-42.

word and action. At one time different church buildings were used for each part. Both parts help us recover the past events which are recited or reenacted. To reverse the name of the children's game, tell and show becomes the sequence. The offertory is the hinge between the two parts. They remain distinct and yet they complement each other.

Our second consensus is as to the basic contents of the service of the Word. Its essence is the recital of a portion of salvation history mingled with praise to God for his works. To these are added a contemporizing of the scriptural witness in the sermon plus intercession for the contemporary action of God. There have been differences in the number of scriptural lessons read and as to whether they were interspersed with psalmody, hymnody, or other forms of praise. But the basic pattern is the telling forth of what God has done with, in effect, a refrain: "Sing to the Lord, for he has risen up in triumph!" Both the sermon and intercessions are integral parts of the Lord's Supper. They reflect the scriptural memories in terms applicable to modern life.

Other strata have been added to this essential outline of the service of the Word. The bare bones can be glimpsed in the synagogue service in Nazareth as narrated in Luke 4. Subsequent accretions include an introductory rite comprised of penitential elements and praise and, at another place (in the West), the Nicene Creed. The West, particularly Protestantism, had a tendency to emphasize the penitential elements as if what really mattered here was the evil man had done rather than the good God had done. But the essential structure of the service of the Word remains today: (introduction), lessons interspersed with praise, sermon, (creed), and intercessions. All these are verbal forms, spoken or sung. The only exception is the kiss of peace sometimes connected to the intercessions.

The third consensus is as to the basic contents of the service of the table. These revolve around actions, what is done rather than what is said. We shall follow the discussion of Gregory Dix regarding what he calls the fourfold shape of the eucharist.[16] This may be an arbitrary limiting of the number of actions involved but Dix's essential insight, that the service of

[16] *The Shape of the Liturgy* (Westminster: Dacre, 1945), pp. 48 ff.

the table is primarily action, is certainly valid. The four actions are suggested by the verbs in the New Testament accounts (Luke 22:19; Mark 14:22; Matthew 26:26; I Corinthians 11: 23-24) and appear in virtually all early liturgies.

The meal begins with the taking, i.e., the preparing, of the food and drink. This is often called the offertory when bread and wine are taken and placed on the Lord's table. Act two is the blessing which to the Jewish mind was the same as giving thanks to God. It is primarily a verbal act though often accompanied by hand gestures, "the manual acts." Giving thanks forms the very center of the whole service, as indicated by the name eucharist (thanksgiving). Third comes the breaking of bread, a practical act when a single loaf is used but a most meaningful symbolic action too. It makes it possible for that which is one to be shared in by many. The final act is the giving of the bread and wine to the congregation. That which has been taken, blessed, and broken is now given back to the communicants. (We shall consider the sign value of these four actions in detail in Chapter VII.) Subsequent growth added various commemorations and devotional material, especially before and after the communion of the people. But none of these are nearly so basic as the four actions and the later accretions have been discarded in many new rites.

Perhaps the most important consensus of all is as to the contents of the giving of thanks, act two of the service of the table. Though there has been a fantastic variety of ways of expressing the contents, beneath is a remarkable unanimity in content throughout twenty centuries of diversity. The essential contents may be defined as follows: (1) an introductory dialogue between clergy and people; (2) a thanksgiving to God for his works (a thanksgiving which may take a fixed form or vary from time to time); (3) a narration of the institution of the Lord's Supper; (4) a remembrance of Christ; (5) an offering to God; (6) an invocation of God's (especially the Holy Spirit's) blessing on the bread and wine for the benefit of the congregation; (7) and a concluding doxology.[17] Frequently this is followed by (8) the Lord's Prayer.

[17] Cf. Cipriano Vagaggini, The Canon of the Mass and Liturgical Reform, trans. by Peter Coughlan (London: Geoffrey Chapman, 1967), pp. 90-91.

The contents may be arranged in various forms, spoken as a monologue or combined with congregational acclamations. In the Church of England and Methodist traditions, parts 5-7 were postponed until after the communion of the people, and the Reformed tradition has placed portions before or after the prayer of thanksgiving. But in the majority of Christian liturgies ever since Hippolytus the sequence may be found, more often than not, as outlined above. This is the basic articulation of the meaning of the Lord's Supper, and though the contents may be expressed in an infinite variety of ways, it would be irresponsible deliberately to ignore its parts. And it is not much more excusable to ignore them out of ignorance. Some very creative canons in the *Underground Mass Book* manage to combine relevancy and authenticity on the basis of this contents. We need a knowledge of history in order to know how to give thanks at the eucharist just as we need a knowledge of Scripture in order to preach. Its contents must be mastered before one can experiment significantly with the eucharist. Failure to do so has often produced eucharistic prayers of sentimental or pietistic nature.

In four areas, then, there are basic agreements as to the structure and contents of the Lord's Supper. A knowledge of these is the first step in liberating the Lord's Supper.

IV

Our fouth and final basic element of worship is the most verbal of all, the divine office. It is usually the normal preaching service in Protestantism. Curiously it goes under many names: divine worship, matins, morning prayer, morning worship, or the "eleven o'clock." All forms of Christian worship employ verbal communication to a greater or lesser degree. This is only to be expected since speech is the most frequent and precise form of human communication, even when combined with other media. Since this is the way people live, it follows that it is also the way they worship. The office is built on verbal communication with little emphasis on the use of action and matter. Thus it is a distinct tradition from Christian initiation or the service of the table in the Lord's Supper.

The divine office has the special ability of covering a wide range of material with the least equivocation. It is ideally adapted to the narration of events plus the repetition of discourses and dialogues. Its showing forth is done by articulation with less ambiguity than other media. Though there is a degree of ambiguity in words, the visual and kinetic media often have far more, and they can hardly cover the range of time and space that the spoken word does. The word can conjure up images of captivity in Babylon, trace the journeys of Paul, or recover a dialogue of Jesus and his disciples, all with a minimum of effort. And there will be considerable unanimity in the insight it communicates to the hearers.

But the office usually treats salvation history in a more leisurely fashion, bit by bit, week after week. Its presentation is cumulative. Episodes of scripture are read and expounded week after week in serial form. The result is a complete and detailed presentation of salvation events in a composite picture, filled in by weekly installments.

The structure of the divine office comes to us through two parallel patterns: the service of the Word from the Lord's Supper and the divine office itself. Ultimately both are derived from the pattern of synagogue worship with its affinities to the educational and social life of the exile community and its mission of keeping Israel alive even while singing "the Lord's song in a foreign land."

We have already encountered the service of the Word as part of the Lord's Supper. Under such names as the mass of the catechumens, fore-mass, ante-communion, synaxis, the service of the Word has stood as part of the Lord's Supper from earliest times. Justin Martyr tells us that there were readings from the scriptures "as long as time permits" in the church in Rome during the second century.[18] With the coming of the Reformation, the Lutheran and Reformed traditions adopted the service of the Word for congregational worship even when the rest of the Supper of the Lord was not commemorated. The new Presbyterian and United Church of Christ liturgies consciously return to this pattern. The offertory and benediction are borrowed from the Lord's Supper to com-

---

[18] *Early Christian Fathers*, p. 287.

plete the services which are, for all purposes, truncated observances of Holy Communion.

The development of the divine office is a bit more complicated, though almost equally important. One has to know the purposes these services served before he can understand the form they took. Apparently they began as Christian prayers of private devotion as we have seen already in Hippolytus.[19] Early in the fourth century, Egyptian monastics, most of whom were laymen, began to develop services based upon the Psalter, plus lessons from the Old Testament (Epistle and Gospel on Saturday and Sunday), and prayer.[20] With the coming of the end of persecution in the fourth century, similar services began to develop in parish churches for all the laity, especially early in the morning and in the evening. Monastic communities both East and West took the lead in developing this form of worship, and Benedict in the sixth century rounded out for the West the eight daily and nightly hours of the divine office. For a thousand years the office remained chiefly a clerical and monastic pattern of worship, till Thomas Cranmer and Martin Luther liberated it in the sixteenth century and returned it to the worship of the laity, whence it had originally sprung. The sermon, offertory, and benediction were borrowed from the Lord's Supper and the office became, what Cranmer never intended, the basic pattern for congregational worship throughout most of Anglican history and the model for Methodist worship. Thus its history is private, public, clerical-monastic, and public again.

Though in many ways similar to the pattern of the service of the Word in the Lord's Supper, the needs of monastic worship have made a major imprint on the divine office, especially in the centrality of the Psalter. The monks intended to recite the Psalter weekly (Anglicans monthly), and so the Psalter came to be a major part of the office. Since the office did not include a sermon, legends of the saints and extracts from homilies by the Doctors of the Church were added. Great

[19] Cf. Juan Mateos, "The Origins of the Divine Office," *Worship* XLI (October 1967): 477-85 and "The Morning and Evening Office," *Worship* XLII (January 1968): 31-37.

[20] John Cassian, "The Institutes," II, 6, in *Nicene and Post-Nicene Fathers*, Sec. Ser. (New York: Christian Literature Company, 1894), XI: 207.

variety in hymnody developed. Since there were eight services each day, prayers fitting the time of day (such as confession for the day's sins at compline) were developed, the whole accomplishing the sanctification of each day in the life of the community.

The essential contents, though, remains the same as in the service of the Word from the Lord's Supper. God's actions are recited from Scripture and praise resounds. Prayer of various types is offered—confession, petition, and intercession particularly. Psalms, canticles, and hymns testify to the works of God which they glorify. It is, throughout, a verbal recalling and rejoicing in what God has done.

V

We have surveyed the four elements of Christian worship that have endured for twenty centuries. Their endurance points to certain constants, not just in liturgical history, but in human life itself. If they had survived only because of inertia we could have skipped this chapter. But we submit that the time cycles, initiation, Lord's Supper, and the divine office have endured because, despite all the changing conditions of human life, they ring true to man's nature.

Since they have endured so long under such varied conditions, we do not expect to see them disappear in the future. The outward expression of these elements will continue to change. This is not to say that other basic elements may in time appear. The canon, like that of Scripture, is theoretically still open, though we are not holding our breath in either case. The four elements may be supplemented, but we do not look to see any of them abandoned. They will, we hope, be better understood and more effectively used than at present.

Actually, these four elements open up such vast possibilities that we are far from exhausting them. They lie as deep as all the forms of communication humanity now knows. It is best to explore what we already have—the given of Christian worship. As humanity changes we must adapt the outward forms, though it is often the most recent accretions that need to be scraped away. And since human life will continue to change, innovation must proceed. The centuries in which human life remained relatively unchanged where periods of slackening of liturgical creativity. Periods of rapid social change demanded increased liturgical adaptation. As people change, the forms of liturgy change, but as some things (Shakespeare's seven ages of man, for example) nevertheless remain little changed, so the hard core of Christian worship endures.

Very often the oldest ingredients prove the most flexible and adaptable. Sometimes an old actor can play new roles more readily than a neophyte. If the reader thinks this is conservatism, then he has got the point. But it is also our conviction that such a conservatism is the only sound basis of radical renewal and development of Christian worship.

The rest of this book is an attempt to show the ways in which the pastoral, theological, and historical norms can be fulfilled by using the media of the modern world. We hope that they will demonstrate the lasting vitality of the elements of hard-core Christian worship even while explaining forms of worship new and unfamiliar to many Christians.

Since the media of communications in our time have changed and have changed human life with them, we shall have to rethink much of Christian worship in terms natural to the man of our times. Above all, we hope to help the reader develop greater sensitivity to what is happening around him, so that he can understand the given of Christian worship and adapt it for our times.

IV

THE ENVIRONMENT OF WORSHIP

In recent years many sensitive Christians have become critical of the expenditure of large sums of money for building churches. During the 1960s construction of religious buildings was a billion dollar annual enterprise in America, but the expenditure for building projects dropped rather sharply toward the end of the decade. A high of $1,285,000,000 in 1961 had declined to $949,000,000 by 1969 but, in terms of increased building costs and inflation of the dollar, this represents a drop of over fifty percent in actual building.[1] No doubt part of the decrease was due to tight money and purely economic problems.

But undoubtedly a major factor was the realization of many Christians that too often church buildings have failed to reflect the nature of the church itself. Often vast monuments have been erected that hardly give the image of a servant church. Many church buildings look more like earthly mansions than servants' quarters. The monumental mentality has been slow in dying, since it reflects a long tradition of a social reality in which the church actually dominated village society in medieval Europe or colonial New England. But bishops are no longer princes, and even village pastors hardly rule their flocks today. The monumental image is no longer genuine, and it reflects a reality we do not seek to recover.

Others criticize the building of churches because of the great expense of money and energy such efforts consume. They

[1] Data from George Christie in *Guild for Religious Architecture Newsletter* No. 86 (October-November 1970), p. 2.

argue the church could better expend its resources in ameliorating society, and that bricks and mortar are a luxury that the church, when true to its mission, can no longer afford. There are too many examples of church plants that have become the country clubs of the middle class to make it possible to ignore this criticism. It is no wonder that building churches is condemned as an unconscientious waste of money, especially when one realizes how many years the resources of the congregation go into paying off the mortgage.

A further criticism is that church buildings impose such a great commitment to ecclesiastical housekeeping. The church becomes identified with the church building, and many of the congregation's activities become ingrown and self-centered because the building has helped isolate them from other human societies. Much activity goes into the maintenance of the property instead of more worthwhile projects. A building-centered program can often be condemned as a needless luxury.

All these criticisms are just. But there is a deep danger in them that they will blind us to just how important the environment of worship is in defining its meaning for the worshipers and in determining the forms of worship that are possible or impossible. One can worship God "in spirit and in truth" anywhere at any time, but it is also true that where and when one worships will have a great deal of effect on his understanding of worship. It is certainly likely, given the existence of over three hundred thousand churches in this country, that most services of Christian worship will continue to be held in these buildings. We must take seriously the environment of worship if we are concerned about its reform.

By the environment of worship we mean the interior of the church (or other building) together with its total contents, including people. Unfortunately churches are usually photographed empty of people, thus missing the most important single aspect of a worship environment. The environment of worship is shaped by a great variety of sensory inputs. These include not only those things that can be seen, but also the way sound behaves in the building, how things feel to both hand and eye, the smell of the place, and the temperature. Lighting, color texture, shape, all affect the way the environment impinges on our consciousness. The furnishings and works of art are important parts of the environment.

The environment of worship (or of any other activity) has a great effect on our feelings, reactions, and thoughts. It rarely provokes conscious and deliberate attention, but it is nevertheless an important factor in how we understand worship. When one begins to experiment with the various environments in which his daily life takes place, he soon begins to realize how thoroughly he is manipulated by his environment and how little he can do to fight back. Take, for example, a busy city freeway where one is surrounded by people whizzing past in cars and yet has no way to communicate with any one of them. Contrast that with a peopled place such as a downtown sidewalk at noon on a pleasant day. The more one tries to control such environments, the more he realizes how much his reactions are determined for him by the givens of the situation. A country location, a private home, a dentist's office, all these have other givens that alter one more than he alters them. One is confounded by the way he is controlled and the difficulty, in so many situations, of fighting back against his environment. How much can one change by shouting, pushing, or stamping his feet in many locations? If a person blocks out one sense at a time (particularly seeing), he soon becomes aware of how much he is manipulated by the things he sees, touches, hears, or smells. It often requires the trained imagination of an architect to make one realize how he can alter his environment, how he can fight back and control the situation rather than be controlled by it.

The architectural setting of worship is a most important component in defining what worship will mean for us. But we must remember that we rarely encounter raw architecture. The building is full of furnishings, decorations, and people. It is heated, lighted, ventilated, and mechanically controlled space. We cannot act as if all our sensory inputs were to be disregarded and say that church architecture is unworthy of the attention of a church engaged in mission to the world. That is, we cannot do this without trying to be less than human. Indeed, if Christians had taken seriously more often how their environment affects their worship, we would have spent far less money and time on buildings that fail to communicate a relevant image of the church.

The interpretation of worship that many church buildings impress on our minds is far from desirable. Many churches give a not-so-subtle indication that the church is the clergy, that there is a great distinction between those who serve about the altar-table and those who merely occupy the pews. We have conspired to separate clergy and people, to elevate the clergy, and to give the impression that worship is a professional sport rather than an amateur one. Removing the choir from the rest of the congregation only serves to exaggerate this professionalism. Some newer buildings, sensitive to the perils of clericalism, inculcate a much more scriptural image of the church as all the people of God, not just the paid staff.

Too often church buildings tend to exalt the role of the church in contemporary society. I once heard Pope Paul VI preach a sermon against triumphalism, but St. Peter's Basilica shouted him down. Vast elegant spaces hardly proclaim the life of a servant people.

Nor can we approve of church buildings that strongly suggest that God is up in the dim recesses of a remote chancel, or worse, out beyond the east window. God is there, all right, but he is in the midst of his people. Emmanuel has come, God is with us. Relevant church architecture avoids a false sense of mysteriousness, in favor of expressing the basic biblical mystery, God present in and with his people.

A church building can be a very important factor in shaping our understanding of what it is to be the church and what it is the church does when it worships. We have placed environment first in our discussion of new forms of worship because it is such an important factor in giving meaning to what we do in worship. Churchill is often quoted as having said that we shape our buildings and ever after they shape us. This is especially true of church buildings. A whole generation's concept of worship is shaped by the building it builds for worship. We used to burn heretical books, but heretical buildings are equally dangerous and would make more spectacular blazes. We must not underestimate the importance of the environment of worship. J. A. T. Robinson has said: "The church building is a prime aid, or a prime hindrance, to the building up of the Body of Christ. . . . And the building will always win." [2]

The environment of worship also prescribes the forms of worship that can be used. This is true, of course, with traditional as well as with new forms. When the building is so reverberant that the preacher's words echo back at him, preaching is nearly impossible. An overly absorbent building soaks up sound so completely that everyone seems to be singing a solo and soon quits. Acoustical environment cannot be neglected.

Unfortunately, many churches impose other forms of restraint. In the average church the furniture is all attached to the floor, and the levels of the floor are all permanently fixed. The buildings are always the same, though it is obvious that they are used for different types of worship, for congregations that vary in size, and on diverse occasions. Not only do the buildings restrict the types of worship presently used, but they thwart future developments. Such buildings tie knots in the future. They stubbornly challenge any alternate forms other than those for which they were originally designed, and even for these they are not always felicitous. The design of the building determines the forms of worship that may be tried.

Suppose one wants to use congregational movement in worship, but the side aisles are too narrow for more than one person to wiggle by at a time. The possiblility of a congregational procession is almost nil. Or one may wish to project some images, but there is no flat surface, or the light cannot be controlled, or there are no electrical outlets. So that project has to be scrapped. One may wish to have the communicants stand around the altar-table, but it is built solidly against the east wall and hemmed in by choir stalls. This possibility, too, falls victim to the building's rigidity. All these are perfectly reasonable expectations but impossible in many church buildings, especially the most expensive ones.

Most church buildings reflect the values of middle-class society. Such edifices stress comfort and security, providing shelter from change or direct involvement for the great silent

[2] *Making the Building Serve the Liturgy,* ed. by Gilbert Cope (London: A. R. Mowbray, 1962), p. 5.

majority. But this is not adequate for new styles of worship that demand direct and full personal participation. Our churches must open possibilities to us rather than exclude them.

And this is quite possible. Good planning can create environments that invite new possibilities. There is no reason why a church building should tie knots in the future. As long as we accept the likelihood of change in the church, as in all life, we can create environments that aid the process of change rather than oppose it. In any case, the building is likely to win, so it is best to have it working with the church rather than against her.

I

It is necessary, then, to spell out just what are desirable criteria for church buildings, so that those building new churches or remodeling old ones may be guided. It seems safe at present to assume that most public worship will continue to take place in church buildings. Later we shall discuss worship in other locations. What is desirable in worship space in the 1970s? Obviously one cannot give specific prescriptions since individual congregations and their needs vary so much. But it is possible to present general criteria by which the adequacy of all church buildings for use in the 1970s may be judged.

We shall propose four general criteria: *utility, simplicity, flexibility,* and *intimacy.* Though we shall discuss these individually, we must keep in mind that all are closely related and that none can be ignored in shaping the space and contents of church buildings for the 1970s.

It is a truism of modern architecture that any building ought to be shaped by and reveal the uses to which it is put. The important thing about a building is the quality of life lived within it, that is, the uses it serves. A church is no different in this sense from other buildings. A church building ought to be shaped by and reveal the uses to which it is put.

1. Our first criterion, therefore, is *utility.* This may seem obvious. Unfortunately it is not to many building committees. Instead they approach their job with a concern about how the

building is going to look rather than how it is to be used. As a consequence, many churches are built for almost anything but their prime function as the setting for Christian worship. We all know of new buildings where orderly means of receiving communion are almost impossible, or weddings can be held only with inconvenience, or where caskets cannot be moved in or out of the main door. A preconceived formalistic concept has been imposed on the building. The building determines its uses rather than the uses shaping the building. It is as if a pattern had been imposed on the congregation rather than the pattern evolving out of their needs. A formalistic approach may produce church buildings splendid to look at but horrible to use. And churches are built primarily to be used, not as scenery. This is not just a question of style. Many a so-called contemporary structure is just as formalistic as one whose form is dictated by Georgian symmetry or the structural limitations of gothic trusses or vaults.

The heart of the formalistic problem is the failure to take seriously the chief use a church building has, that of providing the setting for public worship. Usually this failure occurs because the congregation does not think through seriously what it does with a church building, that is, how it uses space in worship. The primary responsibility of the congregation is to discuss and state in detail the uses to which the building will be put in worship. This is basically a theological endeavor though it does entail consideration of the historical elements of Christian worship. When this effort is not made by the congregation, the architect can only rely on his own imagination as to what the church is and does.

The congregation and its representatives in the building committee must work out a basic understanding of worship in general and then proceed to discuss specific acts of worship. One talks worship before he talks architecture. This will take time, a lot of time. At least two years of preparation should go into preparing to build. The building is going to be around a long time, and time spent in preparing to build is not time wasted. It may, indeed, turn out that the process of preparing to build is more important than the building itself. In many cases it has been a period of renewal for the congregation as it discovered the meaning of its life together.

Churches are built to be used, not to be admired. A common pitfall is a romantic reliance on symbolism, a baneful inheritance from the romanticism of the nineteenth-century gothic revival. We do not put in three windows for the Trinity or two candles for the two natures of Christ. We put in three windows because we want a certain quantity and quality of light and two candles because we need two-candlepower illumination. Churches deliberately planned to resemble a ship, a crown of thorns, or a fish are apt to be romantic curiosities rather than serious architecture. Such visual symbols have often been by-products of a vital function and often were not noticed until the original function had long been forgotten.

Utility is our first criterion and not an easy one to resolve. The uses of no two churches are identical any more than are the congregations. Different people use each church in different ways, and consequently no two churches are exactly alike. We build for the distinctive uses each congregation makes of its building rather than for an abstract concept of ideal functions.

2. Our next criterion is a call to essentials and the elimination of the superfluous. This is the criterion of *simplicity*. Mies van der Rohe's famous principle, "less is more," expresses this well. He meant, of course, that a building refined to its basic essence makes a stronger statement than one cluttered with ornamental details. His 1952 chapel at Illinois Institute of Technology is clean and strong, devoid of the slightest attempt at decoration.

It is difficult in most church buildings to distinguish what is essential from the nonessential. The buildings are so full of furnishings and accessories that we lose sight of the basics. As a communication medium, the average church projects an image of considerable confusion. Devotional, liturgical, and purely utilitarian elements are heaped together with no sense of priorities. Much of this clutter is composed of nonessentials, and as a result the buildings give ambiguous statements of their purpose. Many recent churches would have been greatly improved by restraint in decoration and furnishing and by more discernment as to what is primary in worship. It may sound paradoxical, especially to pastors who have labored so hard to raise money, but many a building project has been wrecked by too large a budget. Some of the most effective church buildings in the last decade are results of an architecture of poverty where financial necessity forced the architect to concentrate only on essentials. "Less is more" when one knows what he is trying to say and refuses further comment.

But what is essential? Actually Christian worship does not demand a very elaborate setting. It began in private homes and some of the most interesting experiments in our time have returned to the house church. All the equipment that was required in early times was a table, a reading stand, a chair for the chief celebrant, and a pool of water for baptisms. Since the building was often a private home, the rooms of the house served different functions: baptism, the Lord's Supper, education, and residence. Not much has changed in twenty centuries as far as essentials are concerned. Only three furnishings are really vital: altar-table, pulpit, and font. At most, five spaces are essential: congregational space, processional space, choir space, baptismal space, and altar-table space.[3]

In our discussion on hard-core Christian worship, we indicated basic types of worship: initiation, eucharist, and the divine office. Baptism demands a container for water, and this is all a font is though one might never guess it to look at many fonts. The Lord's Supper (like any meal) demands a table. Since the Scriptures are always read and expounded at such services, there is a need for a pulpit to hold the Bible and sermon notes. The readings in the divine office require the same pulpit. Anything else is unnecessary. A lectern beside a pulpit suggests a division between the Word read and preached that is not theologically admissible. Prayer desks and communion rails are nonessentials since prayer can be offered at the altar-table, and all one needs to kneel is a step or cushion. People certainly ought to be willing to help the elderly and pregnant kneel. Some would claim that a chair for the chief celebrant from which he can preside over the service—president's chair—is an essential. They argue he needs to maintain eye contact with the congregation throughout the service. (Some of us have not been convinced and

[3] For more detail, see my *Protestant Worship and Church Architecture* (New York: Oxford University Press, 1964), pp. 34-50.

prefer to sit with the congregation except when we need to be on our feet.)

We must also think in terms of space. In a church building, space can be defined by many things besides walls: by lighting, suggestion of enclosure (such as railings), change in floor levels or flooring materials, furnishings (especially pews), and other means.

The most important space in the church is determined by people: congregational space. Too often we have treated this space as if it were the house, the audience space, in a theater. But this is where most of the acting should be. Congregational space is the basic space of the church, the place of meeting. In the Quaker meetinghouse it is the only space.

An important part of worship is movement from place to place, and this demands processional space. This ought to be apparent in churches that receive the Lord's Supper around the altar-table and in all churches at weddings and funerals. All services involve a coming in and going out of the congregation though we have paid comparatively little attention to expressing architecturally the meaning of assembling for worship and going forth for service. Space for movement is likely to be far more important in worship in the future.

Choir space raises particular problems. There is first of all the unresolved question of what are the functions of the choir in Christian worship. Until this is settled to the satisfaction of each congregation, the location (or even the existence) of this space remains highly problematic. There are the additional complications of placing the choir both near the organ console (if any) and where acoustically the singers can be most effective. Locating the choir is one of the most difficult problems in church design today because of our failure to define the choir's functions.

The pulpit hardly needs space about it since it often provides its own internal space for the preacher. The font is different for it is the focus of assembly for a number of people. The minister, the candidates for baptism, and the parents and sponsors of infants meet at the font. A distinct baptismal space is necessary, located where it is visible to the worshiping congregation.

The need for space about the altar-table is more obvious

since the ministers need to stand or kneel behind it. In many churches, communicants also kneel or stand about the altar-table so this space must be readily accessible. Often the amount of this space and its arrangement will determine the length of the communion service.

And that is all. These are the essential furnishings and spaces. It is not even necessary to have seats for the congregation. The church had none for over a thousand years. But these essential furnishings and spaces are needed. They are the hard core of church architecture. Their symbolism is not an afterthought; it is in the way that they are used. Their purposes should be obvious and direct.

Simplicity demands the most honest and direct provision for the purposes the building is to serve and no more. Quite possibly the best buildings erected in the past for worship as it is becoming today were the Shaker meetinghouses of the late eighteenth and early nineteenth centuries. They were plain, simple rectangles with the floor space left open so as not to interfere with dance in worship.

3. Our third criterion is that of *flexibility*, the ability to adapt for different services, congregations, and occasions. Unfortunately, most churches are built as if every service of worship were identical, as if the attendance at all services were the same, and as if all Sundays were alike. They reflect the manufacturing mentality: one product, take it or leave it. But we know that churches never operate this way and are even less likely to do so in the future. A wedding is not holy communion nor is holy communion a sacred concert. Easter is not Thanksgiving nor even Maundy Thursday. Most churches are arranged for the maximum number of people present, and a church that is half full is also, depressingly so, half empty. Our churches need to be flexible in order to adapt to the type of service, the people, and the occasion.

Of course this means compromise. Ideally one would have two different buildings for the Lord's Supper. The service of the Word is directional, someone speaking to others. It demands an arrangement something like a family gathered *in front of* a television set, and the prototype is the synagogue. The service of the table, on the other hand, is concentric. It reflects the family gathered *around* the dining table and goes back to the upper room. Most Protestant churches have been designed for preaching and, since the voice carries in a straight line, the buildings have a horizontal axis. Some recent Catholic churches have been shaped around the altar-table, even designed on a vertical axis. It is difficult to preach to people behind or to the side of the preacher. Essentially a church must be built for both the service of the Word and the service of the table, and this involves compromise between the directional type and the central type, between a preaching church and a sacrament church.

In most churches everything but the people is nailed down. Almost all the open space of the building is filled up with pews and other furnishings, few of them movable. It is amazing what possibilities begin to open up when movable furnishings are introduced. Perkins Chapel is an expensive, rigid, conventional neo-Georgian building with a divided chancel. Only when we built a portable pulpit, altar-table, and font did we realize how many possibilities were open to us. For a preaching service the pulpit could be placed in the central aisle. With a small congregation it could be placed directly in front of the center of the group. The altar-table could be moved close to the people for communion. At baptisms, the font could be placed directly before the congregation. Only with movable furnishings can one begin to adapt a building to the type of worship and the congregation present. This need not demand much expense. It is surprising what one can do with standard 3/4 inch plywood with the edges mitered together and two good coats of paint.

Vertical flexibility is also desirable. Part of the rigidity of most churches is that the chancel floors are all permanently built, perhaps even in poured concrete. There are many advantages in using movable platforms on a flat floor. These can be cheaply made out of 3/4 inch plywood, 2x6 inch lumber, and screen mold then painted or covered with carpeting or floor tile. In Perkins Chapel we usually use such platforms beneath our portable pulpit and altar-table. In some cases it is possible to stack several on top of one another. The larger the congregation, the higher the elevation beneath the pulpit must be in order for the preacher to be heard and seen by people in the rear. No more vertical separation ought

—91—

to be used than necessary since excessive height can convey a sense of remoteness and authoritarianism more forcibly than horizontal separation. Looking up demands a different head position, more uncomfortable than looking at something on our level though more distant.

Our greatest difficulties with regard to flexibility come with regard to congregational space, usually tightly filled with rigid pews. These give us only one configuration, often the worst one possible. Throughout most of the history of the church there were no pews, and people went where the action was at the time—about the pulpit, font, or altar-table. In some parts of the West, pews first became common in the fourteenth century and people sat down on the job. Ever since then, congregations have lost the fluidity of movement that was once taken for granted. They are now lined up in neat rows like soldiers on parade. It is unlikely that we will see an end to congregations seated for worship. But there are far more flexible possibilities than pews. With movable chairs, one can readily adapt the seating for different services and occasions. Chairs can be spread out to adapt to the size of the congregation, avoiding the impression of emptiness given by unoccupied pews. When a church with pews for two hundred people is occupied by a hundred it is half empty. If slightly less than a hundred chairs are set up for the same people they will go home saying that so many attended they even had to bring in extra chairs!

The distance apart of the chairs is also a factor in communication. Some very interesting studies have been made in "social and personal space and man's perception of it . . . [or] proxemics." [4] This involves the distance that people keep from one another. Americans prefer a certain remoteness, older people much more so than younger. These stated distances affect a whole range of reactions among people and animals. (Swans always keep their distance from one another, seals are the opposite.) Only sideways are distances flexible in pews.

Not just any chairs will do, however. Most church people still suffer from the cheap folding metal chairs in Sunday

[4] Cf. Edward T. Hall, *The Hidden Dimension* (Garden City, N.Y.: Doubleday & Co., 1966), p. 1.

—92—

school rooms. Five needs should be kept in mind in ordering church chairs: comfort, attractiveness, ease in staking, ease in firmly linking them (ganging), and a cost figure per unit comparable to pews. Good church chairs, like pews, are not cheap; that is the only merit of the metal chairs. At the Episcopal Cathedral in St. Louis pews were removed altogether in favor of movable wooden chairs. It was found possible to increase (or decrease) the capacity of the building significantly and to adapt it for a variety of worship and musical occasions.[5]

Actually, seating is not very essential, particularly if one is working with a congregation of youth. They do not resent being close together as an intrusion on personal space. If the floor is carpeted and raised around the sides of the room, youth are often quite willing to sit on the floor. There is a certain exhilaration in dispensing with pews and chairs. No one occupies a private space that he has to defend and recover when he moves. The whole space becomes free and belongs to everyone. As in the early church, the whole congregation is fluid and can go where the action is. It must be pointed out, however, that the early church did not have miniskirts!

Processional space is largely defined by seating. Space for processions can be defined according to need if movable chairs are used. Such flexibility is especially useful when a congregational procession is planned for special occasions.

Choir space, too, demands flexibility especially with the advent of a much wider gamut of instruments in worship. You cannot wedge a cello in between two pews, yet there is no reason why we should not make use of amateur instrumentalists as we do of amateur singers. And the size of the choir will certainly vary, especially for sacred concerts. Perhaps the ideal was realized by Giovanni Gabrieli (1557-1612) in St. Mark's, Venice, where he could place choirs of singers and instrumentalists in a variety of lofts around the church. We do not have so wide an option, but it might teach us the need of flexibility in choir space.

We have spoken thus far about flexibility on the floor of the building. Churches have a third dimension, too, though verticality is often overlooked. Walls are not quite so static

[5] E. A. Soevik, "A Problem in Church Renewal: Christ Church Cathedral, St. Louis, Mo." *Faith and Form*, III (April 1970): 12-15.

as we once thought them to be. Banners, posters, and graffiti can make walls change according to the season or event at hand. The electronic media offer us further possibilities. A wall can change during a service if different slides or colors are projected on it. The possibilities will vary on different textures. A hard smooth white surface will give more clarity, if this is desired, than other textures.

Further possibilities are presented by movable enclosures. In our seminary chapel, this was accomplished by a scrim that completely closes off the chancel, no longer used in most of our services. No longer does the empty void of the chancel fight the intimacy of action out in the nave. A scrim is used in theaters frequently. It is a curtain that is transparent when lit from behind but opaque when all the lighting is on the congregational side. Images can be projected on it from both directions. Since our scrim is twenty feet wide and twenty-nine feet high, a wide variety of moving or still images or color combinations can be projected on it simultaneously. The scrim can be put up in twenty minutes and taken down in ten. It has added a remarkable degree of freedom to the use of a rigid building, and we expect to discover more possibilities through it.

If new forms of worship are to develop, our church buildings must be liberated from rigidity. Protestant churches may not see such rapid change as has happened in the Roman Catholic Church, but change is bound to come. It always has. Our churches need to be flexible enough to adapt to people and their worship, not the other way around. Churches are made for worship, not worship for the churches.

4. Our fourth criterion, *intimacy*, is an elusive one. It is not necessarily determined by the size of the building though that is an important factor. The value of intimacy is in fostering a sense of oneness in participation. Its opposites are isolation and detachment. Certainly intimacy is not wholly determined by the building, but it can play a big role in creating or destroying a sense of involvement and participation. When we feel we are actors on stage, we are more prone to play our parts with gusto than when we see ourselves simply as spectators.

Most churches in the past have been built to accommodate

the Easter crowd. Yet it seems likely in the future that we shall see more services of worship attracting rather homogeneous groups. This means smaller groups of worshipers, and the need for maximum capacity is much less. Multiple services are already common in many large congregations and, as the variety of type of services increases, this is likely to continue. Smaller buildings, used more frequently, make better economic sense as well as having advantages for worship.

Size is not the only factor. Acoustics is important. Some buildings soak up sound so completely that the room is dead and gives a feeling of isolation, particularly to someone trying to sing. Buildings in which space is broken up by excessive vertical separations also give a sense of remoteness from the action. God may be high and lifted up but his altar-table is down in the midst of men, or at least only as elevated as sight lines necessitate. We can learn much from the appeal of the house church where intimacy is so effective in creating active involvement for all the worshipers. The building must focus on the people and what they do in worship, not be an abstract monument for them to clutter.

One of the values of the visual arts is in giving a more human scale to buildings. Art produces a personal scale to which we can relate and helps humanize a building, even a large building, whose size might otherwise negate any sense of intimacy. This does not suggest that art should be applied like wallpaper for decoration. We need to use liturgical art on or near each focus of action—pulpit, altar-table, and font—and in congregational space. By its warmth and interest, art can give a human quality and foster a sense of intimacy in buildings that otherwise lack these.

Above all, the accent should be on people, not on the building. The best buildings for worship call attention to the people, not to the architecture. Like good music, good church buildings step aside rather than force themselves on us by self-assertion. People, at first, often feel a bit awkward in a building that is designed to focus on people. They are used to seeing only the back of peoples' heads. But that is not really seeing people. After a little time getting used to seeing one another face to face, people come to insist on such arrangements and anything else seems impersonal. When we come together to meet God we meet, first of all, our neighbor. That should tell us something about worship itself.

These four criteria, then, are important in shaping churches for worship in our time. Given these four criteria, church buildings can be tremendous assets in helping us offer our worship and in creating new forms of worship. Rather than being an obstacle to change, the buildings can themselves be agents in helping us discover how to "sing a new song to the Lord." Buildings can present to us possibilities of discovery that we never before imagined.

And this is what architecture should do. It can liberate men and help them grow. It can, that is, if it is well planned and based upon utility, simplicity, flexibility, and intimacy. Otherwise, as we all know, buildings can easily become millstones around our necks. The difference is up to the congregation to decide. Will it do the necessary thinking and discussing before it builds or remodels, or will it take potluck on whatever the architect can cook up? We shall see in the following chapters how much is at stake here.

II

It has become increasingly common for groups of Christians to worship in locations other than church buildings. One hears frequently of house churches where groups assemble to worship in living rooms, dining rooms, or even kitchens. Other locations are common too: dormitory rooms, offices, student lounges, dining halls, and meeting rooms in banks and shopping centers. Sometimes worship occurs in the midst of events, on protest marches or picket lines. In such situations, the environment plays a large role in determining the meaning worship has for the participants and the forms of worship that they will use.

For many people, worship comes to have new dimensions when conducted in a location in the midst of their daily activities, such as a private home. Worship offered among everyday surroundings loses some of the church mystique of grim faces and dead seriousness. There is a solemnity that we have been conditioned to assume when we enter a church. Children know better, much to the distress of their parents.

Once again, we could learn from children. We are not apt to cultivate this church mystique in a private home but are more relaxed and natural.

Worship in such situations can often seem much more relevant to daily life. Canon Ernest Southcott, a pioneer in this type of worship, records people who said they first saw the connection between what goes on in and outside church at house communions.[6] Among closely packed city dwellers, this means a church in their block or a church in their apartment building. Its location varies from week to week, but it is always where people live or work. This may mean worship in the office or the factory too. In such situations worship gains an identity with daily life, not so easily achieved when the rest of life is isolated behind church doors. One discovers that changing diapers and even correcting term papers are forms of the service of God. It is very easy to forget that work and prayer can both be done in God's service. Worship where we live and work helps make this clearer.

Worship in these situations also places it at the heart of natural groups: family, neighbors, dormitory mates, and co-workers. The groups are small and friendly assemblies of people who know one another. Their relations to one another, everyday relationships that we take so casually, can be rediscovered in a deeper sense as relations in which our service of God takes place. In their natural groups, people are more willing to participate freely.

Such situations help us discover that there is no neutral corner in life where our relationships to God and man do not cross. Far from being a remote esoteric function of living, worship is at the very center of life, giving meaning to all that we do. In this sense, it may be less meaningful when crowded off to the periphery, into a church building which we visit only on Sunday. Worship in familiar daily surroundings gives us entirely new perspectives on the relationship of worship to the routines of life.

Worship in nonchurch environments demands a different style. Much that seems reasonable in church seems absurdly formal or even pompous in someone's living room. People are

[6] *The Parish Comes Alive* (London: A. R. Mowbray & Co., 1958), p. 63.

more relaxed and informal in such situations, and the forms of worship must match them or appear slightly ridiculous. Such worship demands a real sensitivity to the situation and an adaptation of every form. Vestments that may make sense in a large gathering may seem silly with a small group. Much instrumental and choral music will be excluded, but a guitar and folk song will seem right at home.

A formal sermon to a small group in a dormitory room may be an absurdity, but it is a natural opportunity for an open-ended sermon with spoken witnesses from all present. The usual prayers may seem silly in such a situation but it is a wonderful chance for people to offer prayers of petition and intercession themselves. There is an element of spontaneity in a worshiping group in a home environment that we would love to achieve in a large congregation situation, impossible though that may be.

The great attraction of worship outside churches is that the environment and people present foster a high degree of involvement on the part of everyone. For once, the front seats are full and the intimacy of the situation leaves no spectators. There is a real danger, however. Those who have rejoiced in such patterns of worship may find that the services appropriate for a large congregation in a church building seem remote and cold. They long for the intimacy and spontaneity of the small group and may become disenchanted with the church life of the larger community. Yet there are needs that the larger community fulfills that the small group does not provide. The parish has greater power for action, contains a better cross section of the city, and resists the development of a spiritual élite.

We do not mean to deny the great attraction of the house church type of worship. But it must relate also to the congregational assembly for worship. John Wesley's Methodist class meetings provided a great form of spiritual discipline for groups of a dozen or so members, but he always saw to it that the class members worshiped with a Methodist society, bringing together the adherents of many class meetings. Similar experiments in our own time need the discipline and wider life of the congregation to round out those of the cell group.

There are times when it is advantageous to move the congregation itself outside the usual church structure to a different location for worship. This gives the opportunity to become more aware of what is essential in our worship, especially when one worships in a social hall or some such space not associated with worship. Once wrenched away from the accustomed frame of reference, one becomes more conscious of his worship, its forms, and their meaning.

It is also necessary in certain types of experimental services that one move to other spaces. If one wants to use the third-century liturgy of Hippolytus with some sense of the original situation, it will be necessary to move into a room without seats and only a table and a chair for the presider. One can gain more verisimilitude by having the men and the women sit separately but may be shocked to discover the relative proportions of the congregation. The attempt to make such a historical liturgy a genuine experience of worship for today demands considerable effort, but it may help people discover why early Christians risked their lives to participate in such a service. The change in environment will be a major factor in helping people think through the totally different situation of persecuted Christians.

The environment of worship is important no matter where Christians gather to worship, in church or out of it. Everyone who plans worship services ought to be aware of how much environment is a major part of the context of worship. Nor can we expect to do much to control our environment until we become aware of its importance to our worship. Otherwise it will control us and often not to our advantage. It is far better to control our surroundings than to be controlled by them.

V

PHYSICAL MOVEMENT

In most Protestant worship meaningful physical movement is minimal. The human body is neglected except for the ears and mouth. Pierre Berton vividly symbolized the defects of the modern church with the phrase, "the comfortable pew." [1] Such a title implies sedentary, sluggish, and motionless congregations. A stranger easily might take home this impression from many Protestant "eleven o'clock" services.

Meaningful gestures, expressive postures, and significant movement from place to place are rarely noticeable in most Protestant worship. The few movements and actions observable are largely of a utilitarian nature—getting there and getting out—or meaningless—the choir procession. Any sense of actions as eloquent forms of communication has been largely lost. Words abound in our worship, but we are too short of breath for much action.

Part of this deficiency is due to the Reformers' abolition of many traditional ceremonies. The actions in worship accumulated in fifteen hundred years were reevaluated and many sifted out during the Reformation. A reason for rejecting many ceremonies was that they were not biblical. In many cases, of course, this was literally true, though it is highly unfortunate that the Bible was looked on as a handbook of worship. English Puritanism, in particular, insisted on a biblical warrant for everything done in worship. This insistence on divine authority for every item in worship amounted to an idolatry of the Bible while crusading against all idolatry.

[1] *The Comfortable Pew* (Philadelphia: Lippincott, 1965).

There is strange irony in this because the Bible itself is so full of accounts of actions being used to communicate. One has only to think of Jeremiah making a yoke or of Jesus placing a child in the midst of a group to illustrate the kingdom of heaven. Worship as portrayed in the Bible utilizes a full gamut of actions from David's dancing before the ark to the domestic meal of the upper room with its strong sense of mimic action. Worship in the temple with processions and sacrifices represents a variety of cultic acts.

There is further irony in that many of the actions the Reformers rejected were dramatizations of biblical events or phrases. The kiss of peace reflects Christ's words (Matthew 5:24). The robe placed on the newly baptized literalizes Paul's injunction to "put on Christ as a garment" (Galatians 3:27) and the baptismal candles call to mind the parable of the foolish virgins (Matthew 25:1). Certainly none of these ceremonies is commanded by Scripture, but all became cultic ways of communicating scriptural concepts through actions instead of words.

As we have seen, the Reformation coincided with popular literacy and a new stress on verbal forms of communication. Words had not mattered to the laity in the Latin mass; they were central in the Reformed liturgies. It is not surprising that many ceremonies were discarded when it was possible to make similar statements in a much more explicit form through a language people understood. The clear gain of a vernacular liturgy rendered superfluous many a gesture. If the people could hear and understand the prayer of consecration, what need was there to summon their attention with a sacring bell? If all could articulate their offering of praise to God, what need was there for incense? Many ceremonies now seemed redundant because their message could be verbalized. The *Westminster Directory* spoke in 1644 of "the many unprofitable and burdensome Ceremonies" which yet remained in the *Book of Common Prayer*.[2]

Of course, many actions were dropped because they seemed to the men of Reformation to have lost meaning or been perverted. Various acts of anointing—at baptism, confirmation,

[2] *Liturgies of the Western Church*, ed. by Bard Thompson (Cleveland: Meridian Books, 1961), p. 354.

ordination, and visitation of the sick—had disappeared in the 1552 *Book of Common Prayer*, largely, it appears, because of fear they had ceased to convey their original "wholesome" meaning to people. Martin Bucer condemned the use of the white robe and chrism at baptism firmly:

> But for some time we have seen the effect produced by the Romish Antichrists and by the impiety innate in all men, by which they continually turn sacred ceremonies for the worship of God into various wicked shows, so that today those signs among the great majority of people serve more for the maintenance and increase of superstition and show than of piety and religion. Now the occasions for these abuses are to be cut out, not retained.[3]

Protestants were not always in agreement as to just which ceremonies were "wicked shows." Many ceremonies fell victim to that overused word in the Reformation, "superstition." Edward VI, it has been well said, was "highly superstitious of superstition."

But there were some losses more difficult to account for. The giving of the peace, though monopolized by the clergy, could under other circumstances have been rescued as a form of reconciliation.

It must, of course, be pointed out that some actions were added as during the Reformation. The Reformed churches practiced setting up long tables in the church at communion time with the communicants seated about them. It lasted until the nineteenth century in Scotland and still exists in the Netherlands. The Anabaptists refused to baptize infants and immersed adults, though their earliest baptisms were probably by pouring. A latter group, the eighteenth-century Church of the Brethren, recovered the practice of footwashing (John 13) and made of this ceremony an eloquent enactment of Christian servanthood. Some Brethren churches also anointed the sick with oil.

But by and large, the Reformation was a period of loss of vast numbers of ceremonial actions that had communicated

---

[3] From *Censura* in *Christian Initiation: The Reformation Period*, ed. by J. D. C. Fisher (London: S.P.C.K., 1970), pp. 99-100.

meaning in Christian worship for centuries. The losses were least among certain Lutheran bodies (especially in Sweden) where conservatism prevailed and most accentuated among the Anabaptists and the English Puritans. Scottish and English Calvinists exceeded all others in the sheer wordiness of their liturgies. John Knox directed that even during the fraction and administration of the bread and cup "some place of the scriptures is read . . . to the intene that our eyes and senses may not onely be occupiede in these outwarde signes of bread and wyne." [4] In avoiding reliance on "outwarde signes" in favor of words read and spoken, the Reformers were more modern for their times than those who argued for the retention of ceremonial. Sixteenth-century man knew what is was to be set free by literacy just as we today know what it is to be confined by it. To men of the sixteenth century, ceremony must have often appeared to be an unnecessary and inept form of communication. We, in the twentieth century, may come to the opposite conclusion.

Occasionally the Reformation perspective has been side-stepped. One of the most fascinating contributions to forms of worship occurred among members of the United Society of Believers in Christ's Second Appearing, commonly known as Shakers. Originating in England in the eighteenth century, the group migrated to America in 1774. By mid-nineteenth century, the followers of Mother Ann Lee numbered about six thousand in nineteen communities from Maine to Indiana. Dance and marching became an important part of worship in these celibate communities. The dance included both slow marches and ecstatic whirling movements and was usually accompanied by singing. The Shakers explained the use of dance in worship on the basis that "every faculty should be used in the worship of God" and agreed "that the physical motions added a still greater dimension to the expression of Prayer." [5] It was finally given up, not because it was an unsatisfactory form of worship, but because the increased age

[4] From John Knox's "The Forme of Prayers" in Thompson, ed., *Liturgies of the Western Church*, p. 304.
[5] Sister Bertha Lindsay and Sister Lillian Phelps, *Industries and Inventions of the Shakers: Shaker Music* (Canterbury, N. H.: Canterbury Shakers, n. d.), n. p.

of the older members during the Shakers' slow decline (only two communities now remain) made it impossible for some to participate. They decided to discontinue the dance "to maintain a perfect union among the members, a service in which all may participate as One."

Other types of movement became prominent in worship on the American frontier during the nineteenth century as a part of the revival system. Revivalism had its origin in an unsophisticated and often illiterate population. To bring these rough people to Christian faith, rough measures were used. Out of the frontier camp meeting came such practices as the mourners' bench where people went to pray for a conversion experience, the sawdust trail that led new converts forward where the preacher could pray for and lay hands on them, and the altar call where any might assemble at the communion rail to indicate their willingness to "come to Jesus."[6] Music always added to the intensity of such occasions.

The presuppositions and actions that the revival system brought to worship in American Protestantism would embarrass most of us today. Revivalism was shallow theologically, but it did have a deep understanding of human psychology. It realized that to move people spiritually it is often necessary to move them physically. If a person makes a "decision for Christ," it is almost imperative to do something, such as getting out of his "comfortable pew" and going forward. Revivalism has to be seen as a profound bit of folk drama, expressing most successfully the religious convictions of its participants.

Today the average Protestant would not be caught dead "coming to Jesus," at least not down the central aisle of a church filled with people. The only place he would display that much public enthusiasm would be at a football game. The "comfortable pew" might just as easily be labeled the "respectable pew." Its occupant is a quite different person from his grandfather or great-grandfather who was brought to Christian faith by revivalism. Of course, most of the pews would be empty today if revivalism had not succeeded marvelously well

[6] Charles Johnson, *The Frontier Camp Meeting* (Dallas: S.M.U. Press, 1955), p. 203.

in christianizing a largely pagan nation.[7] But the forms of worship used by revivalism no longer have much appeal because the main-line Protestant churches are filled with quite different people than those who occupied the pews a few generations back.

We are not the people our ancestors were. We have been buttoned down by the restraints of middle-class good taste. The youth of today are much more aware of this than their parents. Our worship frequently is a mirror of good taste, noninvolvement, of sitting on our hands. Politicians have spoken of the "silent majority"; the term might just as well apply to worshipers in the middle-class white churches. We have not rejected actions because of theological phobias but because they might commit us. Our ancestors might shout "amen" during a sermon. We do not want to get that involved, especially not in public.

Such restraint is by no means peculiar to the way we worship, for it reflects the way we live. Middle-class good taste arbitrates so much that we do. Our actions, in worship as elsewhere, are affected by our cultural patterns. Americans do not use their hands much in talking, and we avoid touching anyone outside our family except for a perfunctory handshake. We keep our distance and keep our hands to ourselves. Other nationalities are not so repressed. When we live in Italy we realize how much more natural a hug is than a mere handshake. The Italian schoolteacher has to touch each child's face as he enters the classroom. How do you teach a child you have not touched? We Anglo-Saxons have eliminated many expressive actions as demanding too great a risk of commitment.

We could learn what we have missed from the black churches. How much more natural it is to tap your feet to the music, to shout your agreement with the preacher, and actually to enjoy worshiping! The blacks call it "soul," and maybe they are right. At least the experience of worshiping in a black congregation can show us how much we whites miss because of middle-class inhibitions.

The result has been that Protestant worship, for the most part, has been cerebral. It has taken very seriously the impor-

[7] Cf. Franklin H. Littell, *From State Church to Pluralism* (Garden City, N.Y.: Doubleday & Co., 1962), pp. 30-52.

tance of words in communicating the gospel and in responding to it. But it has often forgotten that our humanity is not just a matter of disembodied intellects. Our humanity includes physical bodies too, and we are capable of using more to praise than just our ears and mouths. Surely it is time that we realized we can praise God with our feet, eyes, and nose as well. The actions that the Reformation dropped as unneeded or superstitious, or those that middle-class inhibitions make us shun for fear of commitment, deserve fresh consideration. Two wrongs do not make a right.

I

Physical movements can be important means of communicating meaning, and if the church has lost sight of this it is a great loss. Much of our communication in daily life is not verbal but through actions. A baby cannot understand words at all. But who can convince a parent that he is not communicating with his baby and that the child is not responding? Communication between two people speaking different languages is far from impossible. When you are buying something, money almost always talks. There is communication in peoples' faces, their hand gestures, a nod of the head, a whistle, or a cough. A kiss says far more than words.

Modern communications media have made us more conscious of the nonverbal. Television in particular concentrates on action. Certainly words remain a basic form of communication, but the new electronic media take us one step further, for they show us the actions that words describe. Words are no less important than formerly, but they no longer monopolize communication except perhaps in worship.

We often experience a sincerity in actions that words fail to convey. We remember the parable of the son who only said he would work for his father as contrasted to the son who actually did (Matthew 21:28-31). The impact is obvious; actions often speak louder than words.

Several years ago, we employed a dancer to help teach seminarians how to lead worship. She began by placing the students in a circle and then asked the student standing opposite the professor what he thought of the professor. The student stammered out something polite and safe, but while he said it he took several steps backward. The dancer stopped him and asked the class what his body was saying. The point was clear. His body was expressing how he felt about such an embarrassing demand. She went on to say that one might lie with his lips but that his body would never deceive.

Unfortunately most ministers forget this. We may be fervent in our words, but our bodies often communicate indifference or a let's-get-this-over-with attitude. We are obviously not aware of this, partly because we have not thought seriously about our body as a vehicle of communication. Postures and gestures communicate far more than we realize. They do not deceive. When we become conscious of what our body is saying, we soon realize how much effort and training it takes to make it an effective communicator so that our actions do not contradict our words.

There are many times when actions do speak louder than words. It is the nature of physical movements that they involve the body as well as the mind and produce a greater sense of participation. A deliberate use of postures, gestures, and movements from place to place can give a greater intensity to acts of worship. Words can be cheap, actions demand a bit more participation. Actions, too, can degenerate and become meaningless and routine or deliberately be used to deceive. But there is always the possibility that they can lead us to a deeper insight and more expressive response in our worship.

Worship involves our whole being and not just our mind. Only when we take seriously how important the body is as a vehicle of communication in all life do we recognize the need to consider carefully how we can worship with our body. All that is within us can praise the Lord.

II

If physical movement can be so important in worship, how can we make sensitive use of it? This is a large subject; we shall outline general principles and give some concrete examples that may be valid in our time.

Our most important concern about actions is that they express well what they are meant to signify to our particular congregation. The actions used in worship are not private symbols but communal. The same applies to good liturgical art. Such art is not primarily the reflection of an artist's originality and individuality but of the faith of the whole Christian community. Only those actions that can be accepted by the entire worshiping community ought to be considered appropriate. If some physical movements are likely to give offense because of difficulty or association (rational and irrational) we must reconsider. The liturgy belongs to the whole congregation and not to any individual. If the sign of the cross, for example, will raise anxieties, it certainly ought not be introduced without taking these concerns seriously. Not all the weaker brethren live in Corinth.

Even worse are actions that are wholly antiquarian in nature. It is fascinating to rummage around in old liturgical attics. Yet our real question remains: Does something communicate here and now? Undoubtedly many ancient forms (the kiss of peace) can communicate today. But simply because an action is old does not mean it should be raised from the dead. Postliterate man appears to have much in common with preliterate man. He may be a good deal more sensitive to ancient ceremonies than Reformation man was. But this cannot be taken for granted, and in every instance we must question the power to communicate. Modern man prefers soap and deodorants for hygiene and is not likely to respond to grasp any significance in being anointed with olive oil.

Actions must not depend upon arbitrary association. We cannot take for granted that anything will have meaning unless its significance is fairly obvious. The concepts we communicate by means of actions have to be expressed directly and simply. Rarely has a sermon been carefully thought out until it can be reduced to a single sentence with verb and subject. The same is often true of meaningful actions. The ability to reduce our intent to a simple statement is usually a sign of clarity of thought whether applied to preaching or to movement. There is a danger, however, in assuming that actions are simply charades or word games. They are an entirely different medium from preaching, and the analogy ought not be drawn too closely.

Above all, actions must be chosen so that there is a real

congruity of the sign and the thing signified. If it is difficult for people to get from the sign to the thing signified, then the action is meaningless or worse, misleading. Actions that are private, antiquarian, esoteric, or arbitrary are likely to be meaningless. But when carefully used, actions can be good ways of signifying our insight into God and our response.

We begin our survey of physical movement with postures. Different postures in worship are means of indicating one's attitude to what is being done at the time. As the parts of the service vary, so does one's posture: sitting, kneeling, or standing. Of these three, standing seems to be the most expressive. It calls attention to one's respect for that which is greater than himself. If the president of the United States should enter the room, we would stand out of respect for his office. Standing is an objective posture, paying tribute to that which is greater than we. In recent years, there has been a renewed emphasis on standing as the most appropriate posture for many types of prayer and when we receive communion. We stand to address God, recognizing his presence when we pray and when we receive communion.

Kneeling, on the other hand, is a much more subjective posture, expressing humility. It became the normal posture for prayer during the Middle Ages, and it reflects the role of a feudal vassal placing his hands between those of his lord's. Kneeling expresses well prayer of confession in which humility is demanded, though we sometimes forget that God's willingness to forgive sin is even more significant than our bewailing our transgressions. One could also argue that kneeling is the appropriate posture for prayer of petition when one approaches God as suppliant. But it is hardly the position of a son, and standing is at least as expressive a posture for this kind of prayer. For other types of prayer—praise, thanksgiving, offering, intercession—standing seems to provide a more accurate expression. It may well be that the Protestants will succeed in installing kneelers in churches at just about the time that Catholics get them all removed. Actually, standing is less tiring physically than kneeling.

Sitting is less expressive but does reflect concentration on what someone else is doing. It involves the least exertion but relaxes one enough to listen readily. Some people argue that we ought to stand for the lessons from the Gospel, since often the words are Christ's. But this raises a question as to whether his Spirit does not address us throughout Scripture. Sitting seems to be the most appropriate posture during the lessons and sermon. In small group situations the clergy would likely sit to preach, as in the early church.

One can make too much of the importance of postures, and it is possible to overdo Christian calisthenics in a service. But postures do signify our attitude to what is going on and add a further degree of participation.

Gestures are more complex and varied than postures. Most gestures involve the hands which can be as expressive as facial expressions in communicating concepts and feelings. Unfortunately, most of us have never really discovered our hands. In worship we keep them full of hymnals, bulletins, and prayer books. Ministers especially need to get the books out of their hands. Books can usually be placed on the pulpit or altar-table.

We need to discover our hands with as much wonder as a small baby does when its fist blunders into view and the baby coos back at it. The human hand is incredibly beautiful. Take time to look at yours for five minutes. Reflect on how often the Bible speaks of the Lord's hand or the hand of God as giving, heavy, against us, with us, not shortened, mighty, supporting, leading, and wiping away tears. These and many more hand actions provide central metaphors expressing God's acts in dealing with men.

The one hand gesture that we use eloquently is the position of the minister's hands when he gives the benediction at the end of the service. This final blessing is not a petition that God be good to us but a strong declaration of his love. Often the minister says this more clearly and forcefully with his hands raised in blessing than he does with his lips. If only we could use other gestures to communicate as successfully as this one does!

The sacraments, of course, are full of actions, but we shall defer discussion of them until Chapter VII. Gestures are less obvious in preaching services than in the sacraments but more plentiful than often expected. Since the divine office revolves around the reading and preaching of God's Word, there are several acts that focus on the use of the Bible. We need to explore gestures that convey the concept that God speaks to us through the words of Scripture. The Bible ought to be visible where it is read. This is best done with a pulpit that displays the Bible to the congregation except when it is read. Then the Bible can be taken, placed on the ledge of the pulpit, opened, and the pages turned to the readings for the day. After the lections, the Bible can be returned to its place of high visibility. We hope the idea will be apparent (to the preacher as well as to the congregation) that the sermon attempts to express God's Word in contemporary terms. The visible presence of the Bible reminds us that in preaching we listen for God's Word to us here and now through the preacher's words. The gestures involved in taking the book, turning the pages, and replacing it call our attention to the objective nature of revelation preserved through the corporate memories of the church. The pages ought to be turned carefully without hesitation to the place sought. This can be marked by a ribbon. To show difficulty in locating Hebrews communicates to all that one simply has not prepared the service with care, and to fail to find Hosea undercuts any confidence the congregation may have in the minister as a scholar of God's Word.

A sentimental practice such as carrying one's favorite Bible tucked close to his heart, or the opposite, vehemently pounding his fist on the Bible, ought to be avoided. There are bad gestures as well as good ones, and how we handle the Bible often discloses how seriously we take it as source of God's Word. People sense these attitudes even though the minister may not be aware of what he is communicating.

Several other ancient gestures might be considered though they may appear too theatrical for some people. Striking one's breast during the prayer of confession is a biblical gesture (Luke 18:13) that stresses our responsibility for our transgressions. It can be used by both ministers and congregation. The minister might consider the *orantes* position during prayers (other than confession). This is a position, often seen in catacomb art, of a person praying with his arms stretched out toward heaven. Clement of Alexandria speaks of prayer in which "we raise the head and lift the hands to heaven" (*Stromata*, VII:7). Both the early church and eastern religions may help us to think of prayer as involving the body. The *orantes* position would be rather difficult for people crowded into pews.

An ancient practice that commends itself to modern times is the passing of the peace. It is the practice, based on Matthew 5:24, of indicating one's reconciliation with his neighbor before making his offering to God. It combines the vertical (Godward) and horizontal (manward) dimensions of worship. When the service does not include communion, the peace is best placed at the beginning of prayers of intercession, at the offertory, or at the benediction. There are various ways of giving the peace. The oldest tradition was probably a genuine kiss and embrace. This became a stylized embrace with the two participants nodding their heads first over one shoulder then the other.

Today, the peace is most often given with a handshake or double handclasp. The minister usually initiates it with other ministers, then may shake the hand of the person at the center aisle of the first pew, or even of the people at the end of each pew. The peace is then passed down the pew with the handshake or embrace and words such as: "The peace of the Lord be with you" and the response: "And with your spirit." Often the Christian name of each individual is used. Another method is to ask each person to choose a partner before the service begins. He then gives the peace to this partner at the appropriate time. In some churches it is possible for the partners to pronounce forgiveness to each other in God's name after the prayer of confession. To ask that we confess to each other is risky since our partner may be a stranger or the local gossip. Certainly the embrace is the best symbolic gesture of reconciliation. It is natural for Mexican-Americans, and most of us can feel comfortable with it in small-group services. After all, it is hard to love our neighbor if we are not willing even to touch him!

Weddings are occasions when we rely heavily on gestures to indicate meaning. Indeed it would be interesting to conduct a wedding service between two deaf people and see if much were lost by the omission of words. The most obvious gesture is the father giving away the bride, signifying her moving from one family allegiance to another. Though we call it giving away, it is just as much reception on the part of the husband.

This is evident in the clasping of hands as the groom first takes the bride's right hand, then she takes his.

We could improve on the communication a bit if bride and groom faced each other for the exchange of vows. After all, the vows are meant for each other, not for the minister. The couple marry each other, and the minister is only there as prompter and witness. The giving of rings is another gesture whose power is hard to deny. It reflects other symbolic exchanges of property, and illustrates the endowing of the partner with all one's worldly goods. Unfortunately we have become too squeamish to include the second phrase of this act: "with my body I thee worship."

In the case of city funerals, we have lost the central gestures of lowering of the casket into the grave and the casting of dirt upon the casket. The two dominant concepts in Protestant burial rites are the reality of death and the sufficiency of God. We have been lured into avoiding the former for a Christian Science view that conceals the grave and hides the obvious. Certainly our ancestors knew better, and nothing illustrated the reality of death better than the casting of dirt on the casket. We settle, instead, for fake grass and no sign of God's good earth.

Gestures can be deeply moving ways of expressing our thoughts and feelings in worship. We must remember, however, the need for congruity of the sign we use and that which we wish to signify. Some groups have tried various gestures such as swaying back and forth during worship though this seems a purely arbitrary form.

Gestures that seem affected and unnatural may communicate affectation rather than what we intend. Some of the gestures of the old Roman mass hardly seemed masculine and undercut what the priest intended to communicate. Gestures that seem natural can be important ways of strengthening our involvement in worship by adding one more dimension of participation.

Even more important than gestures can be movement from place to place as a statement of intention in worship. We have become so accustomed to immobility in our narrow files of pews that we hardly realize the possibilities of worshiping God with our feet. We have yet to shake off these shackles to realize the values of movement from place to place in worship. For some of us this realization first came through the use of the third-century liturgy of Hippolytus and the effort to reproduce the settings of this worship. With no pews or chairs to enclose space, we found we could sit or stand anywhere, wherever the action was. There was no need to return to the same spot after communion or at any other time. We were not bound to keep "our place."

There are many movements of place in worship that can have meaning. When the minister moves to the pulpit or font or altar-table, he is indicating a change in the pattern of worship. These are not accidental movements, or at least should not be, but mark transitions from the service of the Word to the offering of prayer or other acts of worship. By going to his seat the minister indicates he is turning a part of the service over to the congregation, to musicians, or to someone else's leadership.

In the Church of Scotland it has become common to bring the Bible in at the beginning of a service, place it on the pulpit, then remove it at the close of worship. The practice reflects the ancient little entrance of the eastern churches in which the gospel book is carried in with ceremony immediately before it is read. Some have found the Bible procession a good means of calling attention to the importance of God's Word in Protestant worship. It certainly underlines the presence of God's Word in the midst of his worshiping people. In the Roman Catholic Church, there is sometimes an elaborate procession at the reading of the gospel lesson, and the book is often accompanied by candle bearers. In the Church of Scotland the sexton usually carries the Bible in and out of the church, but it may be done by the minister or, preferably, a member of the congregation.

Movements of the congregation are of much more importance. We have lost some that meant much to our ancestors, such as the old altar call that summoned to the communion rail people who wanted to join the church or to mark a spiritual crisis. We have put nothing in its place, and this bit of spontaneity, despite all the drawbacks of walk-in church membership and spiritual exhibitionism, added a degree of warmth and involvement that we have not replaced. The altar prayers, in which anyone who wished to was invited to come and kneel at the communion rail, have frequently disappeared. But they may have had a real power of expressing that prayer was more than a casual matter, and quite possibly the movement often said more to the people than the words they prayed. Our ancestors knew how to worship with their feet.

We fail to take seriously some of the movements we have retained. When we gather to worship we try to keep people quiet lest they disturb the prayers of others. Maybe the act of people assembling for worship is more important than privacy in saying our prayers. The church is a meetinghouse where men meet as they congregate to worship. Assembly for Christ ought not be chilled in frosty silence, as if that were more spiritual, but be rejoicing in once again recognizing his Body.

Another movement takes place during the offering. Ideally we all ought to bring our gifts forward and place a token of ourselves on the altar-table. This is possible in small congregations. Otherwise representatives of the congregation can take up the offering and present it for us. But why does it always have to be men? Women earn and spend a good deal of money today. And children get a sense of belonging and a certain thrill of status when asked to take the lead in this part of worship. The offering of money is far more than a utilitarian act of getting money for church expenses. It does represent a giving up of some things we would have otherwise had but, in a larger dimension, it is a token of ourselves, offered through the surrender of a bit of property.

At communion, in many denominations, the congregation moves to the altar-table, either to stand or to kneel at the communion rail. One goes forward, not knowing beside whom he will stand or kneel, but discovering anew his oneness with his neighbor through their oneness in receiving from God. There are few acts of worship more eloquent than going to receive communion yet none more difficult to compress into words. We go forward with a sense of offering but discover that it is we who in reality are the recipients of God's gifts. This dimension is scarcely glimpsed in pew communion. When the communicants stand or kneel about the altar-table at the end of their procession forward, we have a model of life as it really is, God giving himself to us that we may give ourselves to one another. And then we return to the same old pews and lives but all is now changed.

The service closes with everyone leaving. It is not simply a matter of exiting. Our worship continues through our work in the world outside. We scatter to continue a service that has only begun in church. Actually we have not done much to make this scattering a very evocative act, and it too often becomes a scramble to the parking lot. The design and location of the building's exits and the placement of banners and graphics nearby can do much to determine any meaning that may be attached to the act of going forth to serve. We glorify God in his world as well as in church, and the way we leave the church building can suggest this.

The congregational procession provides a much more exciting use of motion than we usually risk. In the congregational procession, everyone marches around the inside of the church or outdoors while singing a hymn. Such a procession is a means of affirmation and will be much more expressive than the simple recitation of a creed. It is a form of employing our total being, body and mouth, in affirming what we believe.

Processions are a very ancient form of Christian worship, going back at least to the fifth century. When worshipers became immobilized in pews, processions were hampered though not eliminated till the Reformation. Processions were rediscovered as a form of witness in our own time by those crusading for various forms of social justice. Television has made us all realize what an effective form of witness the marching demonstration can be. It is a pity that the church let go of such a stirring form of testimony. Today the Christian demonstration or congregational procession is reasserting itself as a form of worship.

A procession is not an every Sunday affair any more than birthdays and anniversaries come weekly in families. It is a means of underscoring an important event in the church's yearly cycle of remembering Christ, particularly one of the great festivals of the church year. Palm Sunday is traditionally an occasion for a procession with palm (olive in Italy) branches recalling Jesus' triumphant entry into Jerusalem. All Saints' Day lends itself to processions as do Good Friday (to the cross) and other major festivals. For most of these occasions there are appropriate hymns with a marching rhythm.

A procession is a colorful occasion involving several media. Banners ought to be carried in processions, especially one at the head for people to follow. They must be secured so they do not blow off the pole if the group moves outdoors. Good banners are meant to be carried and are most joyful when in motion. Placards may be made and carried as in demonstrations for social causes. At Easter we once prepared four placards saying "Alleluia" and "Christ Is Risen," and used "Christ the Lord Is Risen Today" as our marching hymn. When we got back into the chapel, we discovered we had ten placards, having been joined by some antiwar marchers. On one All Saints' Day, the congregation met earlier and made placards naming the saints who meant most to them. The sermon was a reading of the calendar of saints for a few months, listing name, century, and occupation. It included St. Thomas, thirteenth century, friar; St. Mary Magdalene, first century, harlot; Dietrich Bonhoeffer, twentieth century, theologian; and many other sorts and conditions, a cross section of the church in time and space. Balloons or sunflowers may be carried (especially by children) or sparklers at night (when a large size can be secured).

The path of the procession will depend largely on the church building. Many churches are so crowded with pews that movement is difficult. It is best to circumambulate the inside of the church. Posters or something visual can mark the turning places. If the weather is good, a procession can go outside and walk around the building. In a church with a central and side aisles, it usually works best for the people to go into the central aisle from either side, form a double line, and march behind a banner. Then, when they come back into the church, the lines split, half going down each side aisle so the people can all slip back into their original places.

A procession is emphatically a time for music. Usually this means that people need to carry a hymnal. The procession should keep moving even though the organist may play improvisations between stanzas. Obviously a good marching tempo should be chosen. If the procession moves outside the church building, it is helpful to have trumpets. Frequently an organ can be heard outdoors if the windows are open, but a trumpet outside is even better. A brass choir, playing Vaughan Williams' tune, "For All the Saints," can be magnificent on All Saints' Day. It is usually best for the musicians to be stationary. Frequently it will be necessary to repeat the hymn once or twice and those with many stanzas ought to be chosen. There is no need for the marchers to keep in step to the music.

Obviously processions ought to be held only on special occasions and not too often. They are exhilarating forms of affirmation, and preaching sometimes seems a weak witness by comparison. The procession can occur at the beginning, middle, or end of the service. Probably the beginning (after the call to worship) is best, between the service of the Word and the communion service next best. It will be necessary to give instructions the first time, and it is particularly helpful to have a banner to follow. Make sure the children do not miss it. They may understand it best of all.

We have some movements that are meaningless or worse. Many churches are so designed that it is difficult for the choir to get to their stalls without going through the congregation. And so we have contrived to make a virtue out of a necessity. There is nothing particularly edifying about seeing a choir tramping through a congregation on their way to the choir loft. Choirs are to be heard, not seen, except when they are trained to lead the congregation in actions. It is all the better if they can slip in and out inconspicuously.

Even worse is when we make a major event of the entrance of the clergy. This may once have had its place when the clergy dominated society, but to have them process in or out with great ceremony is triumphalism at its worst. We have no need to exaggerate the importance of the clergy, and they can get to work, like the rest of us, without the accompaniment of cross and candles. In many cases, the presiding minister could very well sit with his family until the service begins and then take the few steps to the chancel from there.

Movement from place to place can be a genuine and meaningful form of worship if the movement has real sign value. It demands the involvement of our total being, not just our intellect, and provides the fullest form of participation. We can worship with our feet.

Clothing dictates our gestures and movements considerably. Anyone who has watched a minister in a buttoned business suit try to raise his arms to declare the benediction will observe how much clothing controls our movements. It does this in many ways that we are much less conscious of than this example. The clothes we wear restrain or encourage, amplify or minimize movements and gestures. Tight fitting clothes make some gestures natural while loosely draped clothes demand others. Long sleeves limit some possibilities, long robes others. The rubrics in the Roman Catholic mass, regarding the priest's actions at the altar-table, make little sense unless one realizes that they are written to direct a man wearing a chasuble that can, from time to time, swallow up his hands. Several of his gestures are dictated not by his words but by his vestment.

Clothing is a form of communication. It may communicate far more than we expect. I once rented a janitor's uniform to preach a communion sermon on how sharing in bread relates us to all men. It was my usual communion sermon, hardly different from several I had preached before. But more people indicated they had "heard" it that day, largely, I suspect, because of the clothing.

Clothing communicates our concept of the occasion in church or elsewhere. How embarrassed we are when we wear the wrong thing to a party and thus communicate to our host that we misunderstood the occasion! We want to wear something that corresponds with the occasion, something appropriate. So we keep on hand several types of clothing to fit different events.

If we were to design the worst possible outfit for church we would probably choose something dark and gloomy. We would then shape it in a form that seemed solemn and archaic, say like a judge's robe (though that might displease the radicals) or like a professor's robe (though that might offend the far right). Then we would make it loosely fitting to stifle movement and add long sleeves to make it doubly awkward. We would end up with what most ministers now wear—the preaching robe. Could anything be more joyless, irrelevant, and awkward?

What should the minister wear? This is not easily answered. Some would say he should wear the same as everyone else, only watch the flowery ties and red socks. This may be right because we do not want to exaggerate the difference between the ministry of the clergy and laity. There is a lot to be said for this on many occasions and, in small group situations, it seems the only sensible answer. But it is a rather negative form of egalitarianism, a reduction to the lowest common denominator.

Perhaps the minister ought to wear something that suggests the depth of consciousness with which we approach worship. It may be helpful in this case to wear something that is not found in everyone's wardrobe and does not reflect the fads of fashion, but a garment that is distinctive and communicates that more is at hand than business as usual. My proposal for most occasions with a large congregation is the alb, a long white cotton-blend garment, rather tightly fitting. Its color is white, about as joyful as we could find for those who rejoice in the good news of the gospel. It can be worn over almost anything or hardly anything and is certainly the coolest clerical garb. Furthermore it is easily washed and is the cheapest (twenty to thirty dollars) of clerical garments. Most important, it places little restriction on the movements of the wearer. Often a white handkerchief (amice) is placed around the neck to hide whatever one is wearing beneath it and a white rope (cincture) tied around the waist. The alb can be traced back to the white tunic worn by men and women in ancient Rome.

Color can be added in a stole worn around the neck. It may reflect the season of the church year by its color or by various symbols. Stoles go back to the early church as a badge of ordained ministry and are not appropriate (though widely merchandised) for choir use. In almost any congregation there are people who will be glad to make cheaper and better stoles than the ones sold in church goods stores. Wools, upholstery fabrics, and many rough materials work well. Decorations may take the form of threads of a different color woven in (in fabrics of loose weave), couched, or embroidered, or appliquéd pieces of cloth.

There are special times in the year when the minister may want to wear something over the alb that communicates the significance of the occasion. The traditional garment for this has been the chasuble. These have now broken out into all kinds of fascinating design opportunities. Just do not try to make it religious. Make it coarse and somber for lent or white or plaid for Easter, or apply braids or anything else. The basic form is that of a poncho. Gestures are easier in a chasuble with a byzantine cut, a full semicircle in back and cut up to waist height in front. But this should not be overdone. A chasuble can be worn on special occasions. Maybe a business suit should be worn the next Sunday. There is no reason to wear the same garb at every service unless we believe every occasion for worship is identical with all others.

The real solution is not to stop with the minister but to dress up the congregation. All present offer worship, not just the minister and choir. Among Orthodox Jews, a prayer shawl is worn by the men at prayer. All the men are equal in this form of clothing. A relatively easy (and cheap way) is to provide the entire congregation with stoles made out of crepe paper, emphasizing the priesthood of all Christian worshipers. Rolls of crepe paper of different colors may be torn at about five-foot lengths or sheaves of it may be cut with a paper cutter. It is extraordinary how the appearance of the congregation changes when all put on stoles. It is even more surprising how it reduces some of their inhibitions about full involvement in the service. This, too, we would do only on certain occasions, but it may be helpful to be as concerned about what the congregation wears as we are about the minister's garb.

Special problems arise with regard to dance. It is, of course, a form of movement from place to place, but it deserves separate consideration. Interpretive dance has been used on occasion in many churches. Usually a group of trained dancers comes and performs during a hymn, anthem, or instrumental piece, or else during the reading of a passage, often from the Bible. The congregation gets a sense of movement simply by watching. We may become involved further if the words are left to our imagination and we are forced to supply our own interpretation of the dancer's intention.

Some will object to dance in the church precisely on this ground. They will find it vague and imprecise because it does not articulate meaning as they are accustomed. This fear vanishes when a text is put into their hands, but then they are substituting another art form. Dance in the church ought to try to express the interiority of reality and not be entertainment. But to make it simply an illustration of a text is to make it a secondary art form.

Others will object to dance because, they say, it is too sexy. Dance often requires very tightly fitting garments. But sex is hardly something irreligious, and Genesis makes it clear it was God's idea in the first place. We are so accustomed to a liturgy composed by celibates for celibates that we forget that sexuality is one of God's greatest gifts. We praise God for everything else he has created but skip past the rather basic fact that he created us male and female. Why can we not glorify God for sex and with sex? The Benedictines certainly did not have this in mind, but "that in all things God may be glorified" ought to include sex.

There is a problem in limiting the dance to those who are trained dancers. Most of us are not musicians, but we try to sing. Neither dance nor music ought to make the congregation only an audience or spectators. It would be better to have the congregation dance when possible. Obviously pews will prevent this, but on occasion we can worship elsewhere or in the aisles. Sydney Carter's adaptation for "The Lord of the Dance" has inspired this in many churches. The music from the movie, "Zorba the Greek," lends itself to a clasping of arms at shoulder height and a swaying motion. It should be clear that this is used to celebrate joy in a particular salvation event, not just for fun.

Some may argue that congregational dance is not nearly so skilled and beautiful as that of trained dancers. But that is to miss the point. We come to worship not to see a performance but to act and respond ourselves. Worship is an amateur sport and aesthetic excellence, though desirable, is not the highest criterion of worship. If one has to choose between artistic excellence or a higher degree of involvement on the part of the entire congregation, the latter would often seem to be the better choice. On certain occasions it might be best for the professionals to perform so that others may learn how to dance in God's service.

We can conclude this chapter by waiving our rule and describing an actual service in some detail. It is a communion service that I have done several times with congregations of seminarians or ministers. It should be made clear from the beginning that this "Silent Service" is genuine worship but is also highly didactic and ought not be used with lay congregations. One can lecture for hours on end on the fact that worship is much more than words. People will write down words to that effect in their notebooks. As so often with regard to worship, there are many things that you can show people but that you cannot tell them. The purpose of the "Silent Service" is to demonstrate how much more there is to worship than simply reading or listening to words from a book or sermon manuscript.

We presuppose that the congregation is familiar with the communion service in the denominational hymnal. Hopefully this can be assumed with seminarians and ministers. As they enter the church, each person is presented a mimeographed piece of paper with the silhouette of a face and finger raised in silence before the mouth. Beneath appear the words: "The Lord is in his holy temple; let all the earth etc." (Habakkuk 2:20). The text below asks the congregation to turn to the communion service in the hymnal and to follow it without any sounds but urging them to use and create their own gestures throughout. They are also urged to create their own sermon from the cues supplied by the preacher.

No sound is made in the entire service. There is no music nor speaking, and this is almost uncanny at first. The minister leads the service by use of postures, gestures, and movements. This necessitates careful study of the service to pick out the verbs. Some are obvious: "Lift up your hearts," or, "Gather up the crumbs under thy table." Others suggest themselves. The opening salutation becomes a wave of the hand to the congregation and a few individuals always catch on and wave back. The service of the Word is not easy, though beating the breast and kneeling at confession and a blessing at the prayer for pardon are helpful. And a gesture can suggest, "Glory be to God on high." Some overacting is necessary.

The sermon is done with various artifacts. One sermon, based on I John 4:8b, involves three words written on pieces of red construction paper: "God," "is," and "love." To these are added a question mark on blue paper and an exclamation point on pink, a poster of a Vietnam casualty, and a crucifix. These seven objects are then held up in various sequences for people to devise their own sermons. Instead of one sermon for two hundred people there are two hundred. I wish I could have as good attention when I preach with my mouth open!

The second half of the service is much easier since it is basically action. After the sermon I change from the black preaching robe into a white alb, hidden hitherto. The change is indicative, as is Norma's change of clothes in Ibsen's "A Doll's House," underscoring the move to the Lord's meal. A table cloth, preferably red and white checked (concealed to this point) is spread on the altar-table and members of the congregation bring forward the loaf of bread and a decanter of wine. The wine is poured (audibly) into a chalice and all then stand. The prayer of thanksgiving (consecration) is emphasized with the *orantes* position and raising the bread and chalice. Then the bread is broken and the people beckoned forward. The service concludes with hands raised in benediction.

Once people have experienced this service they can hardly deny that worship is far more than words. On one occasion, applause broke out but, when I made a gesture of silence, people found they could make the same statement by clasping their hands over their heads. The most affirmative response came when, after the service, a woman ran up to me, hugged and kissed me and then disappeared. It has never happened again but certainly this was a nonverbal response! There are, of course, some difficult parts in the service of the Word, but they only highlight the centrality of the Word in that part of the service. The key thing is the high degree of involvement the congregation feels and their discovery that we have buried the actions of the Lord's Supper under a haystack of words. I know no better way to show people that actions speak louder than words than to deprive them temporarily of words so they can glimpse the importance of action in worship.

VI
SOUNDS AND SIGHTS

Music is closely related to physical movements, though it seems that we have almost managed to forget this in the white middle-class churches. Our children certainly realize this relationship though they are rarely moved by the music they hear in churches. In some black churches, music immediately pulls our body into the act with an infectious foot-tapping rhythm. And out beyond the fringes of respectability (or back a few generations) are plenty of white churches where hand clapping is an acceptable part of worship music. All this we have forgotten, and we deem the pleas for old-time hymns (i.e., rhythmic music) as unsophisticated throwbacks to an age better erased from memory. As a result, we respond to music only with our ears, not with our whole body.

Why then do we bother with music in church if it is so restrained? Why are so much effort and expense given to music in Protestant churches that it consumes far more time and money than all the other preparations for worship except architecture and (perhaps) the sermon? Why is church music frequently a major factor in the choice of a church by people moving into a new community?

The potential of church music, even diminished by our inhibitions, is that it gives a greater degree of intensity to whatever it accompanies, whether words, march, dance, or meditation. When mated with words, the words can gain a greater power of expression unless the two are terribly mismatched. If we use movement, such as a procession, music can be a powerful source of support. In meditation, music can guide and strengthen our thoughts. Music can reinforce our deepest feelings, particularly on such occasions as weddings and funerals. (Music can give greater intensity to what we think, say, and do in worship.) And since we hope to renew and deepen our Christian faith as we worship, music becomes an important part of strengthening the Christian life. Through music its joys become more radiantly expressed, its sorrows more poignantly portrayed. Music can be an important help in deepening our consciousness of reality. It adds another layer of meaning by helping us express the inarticulate nature of reality, the awe and solemnity of (recognizing God's presence) and the joy of lifting up our hearts in thanksgiving. (Music pushes words beyond the normal boundaries of meaning by adding another dimension to them.)

(Music adds a greater degree of participation) (especially in congregational singing.) We not only say the words, we color them in by adding melody, harmony, and rhythm. To the bare words are added variety in speed, pitch, and volume. And thus music is an interpretation of words at the very time they are sung. (Sung words give much more latitude for expression than spoken words.) Once in a while we need to do a service with no music whatsoever just to make us realize how important the music is in coloring the meaning of bare words. The same service, done without music, will seem flat and dull though the words remain identical. Musicians like to say that "he who sings, prays twice."

As our self-consciousness fades, we may find movements more natural as response to music. Tapping our feet, clapping our hands, even swaying to the beat of music can heighten our involvement. And when we are no longer stationary, music will invigorate our movement from place to place.

If participation is such an important part of the function of music in worship, we have further questions to raise. It should be apparent by now that we regard "full, conscious, and active participation" [1] as most desirable for the reform of worship in our time. The demand to be "turned on" is not just a passing catchy phrase but an apt expression of authentic worship in which a person is fully involved. It is the antithesis of

[1] *Documents of Vatican II*, p. 144.

pleasant daydreaming, of casual entertainment, of lukewarm passivity. All these, too, can be and frequently are encouraged by music, most notoriously the piped-in "muzak" of airports and grocery stores. Church music at times degenerates to this level, filling in voids in the service or blotting out the sounds of people whispering and entering late. But this is abuse of music. On the other hand, skillful improvisation may be of real value at the right times.

(Rightly used, music stimulates participation) reaching its fullest degree in congregational song, whether hymnody or service music (doxologies, sanctus, agnus dei, etc.) Not only does the singer participate as listener, but he is performer too, speaking and singing the words. He also usually stands to sing. By contrast, instrumental music or choral music is that of the specialist with the other worshipers less active taking the roles of listeners only. Choir and instrumental music usually demand more skill and are often aesthetically far more beautiful than congregational song.

But here we are back to our old debate about glorification of God and sanctification of man. Choir music, admittedly, is apt to be better music aesthetically than congregational song since it has been rehearsed and the singers (hopefully) have the benefit of at least a bit of training. Far more ambitious types of music may be attempted by choirs than by the congregation. We have made much progress in recent years in training choirs and in selecting "better" music. If God is glorified by "good" music, then it can safely be said that we are doing a better job at it. But what about the sanctification of man?

All too often improvement in choral music has been accompanied by a deterioration in congregational song. Professor Carlton R. Young has remarked that in recent years we have tended to treat the choir as the congregation whereas we should have treated the whole congregation as the choir. (Of course in English cathedral and collegiate churches the congregation and choir were once one and the same on most occasions.) Unfortunately, trained choirs seem to have a tendency to subvert congregational song. There is no doubt that choirs do a "better" job of producing "good" music. It would be nearly impossible to get congregations to sing some of the anthems choirs regularly perform. But is the beauty of music the real criterion by which it is to be judged as (liturgical) music? Certainly we would ask more of liturgical art than beauty. Must not full and active participation be our first concern and beauty a secondary and happy goal?

We must remember that beauty is not a primary concern in worship but a by-product. We are more concerned with the sufficiency and adequacy of the forms of worship to function well, a beauty of proportionality, than of looking for beauty as an isolated abstract ideal. One is tempted to think again of the midwestern grain elevator that was built for only one purpose—to hold grain. It succeeded magnificently in creating beauty, while everyone was trying to beautify his home with Victorian gingerbread. Beauty in worship is a by-product, highly desirable, but not the prime end of worship.

Unfortunately, the professional church musician is threatened by what is happening in worship today. He has worked so long and hard to instill "quality" into worship music that what is currently happening seems a giant step backward. The schools preparing church musicians have worked hard to train people who will know the difference between "good" music and "bad." Meanwhile the liturgists are saying we should look first to what people will sing themselves. Musicians and liturgists seem to be drifting further and further apart, a tragic split though hardly a new one.

Since I am a (liturgist) I am prone to feel that the musician has been a victim of his own musical excellence. Should he want less than the very best he would not be worth his pay, meager as that usually is. But what is best for offering our worship, music of high aesthetic quality or music of a singable and relevant variety? Too long we have operated on a notion that what was best could be distinguished by careful rules. We could say Bach was good and Sullivan was not because of certain standards. But we did not always bother to say good for what or for whom. This led to an aesthetic snobbery that meant we thought we knew what was good for everyone. We adopted a like-it-or-leave-it attitude which is no better in worship than it is in patriotism. How important then are aesthetic standards? They are extremely important in distinguishing between the various possibilities on the same level of musical accomplishment and difficulty. But even more important is the concern that music be for the people. In worship, music ought to be judged in terms of people, not people in terms of music.

This sounds like philistinism, like artistic unlicense. Maybe it is, but I think not. There is still a tremendous amount of discrimination and discernment between what people can sing and what they do in fact sing. Music that people will sing is certainly of different calibers, aesthetically, theologically, socially. The musician has a responsibility to insure that church music is not only "good" in terms of words and music but also in terms of being "good for" people's use. These are not contradictory needs. How do we find music that provides for full and (enthusiastic participation of a specific congregation of people and yet expresses Christian faith?)This demands a more complex type of discrimination and makes our aesthetics functional aesthetics. "Good for" becomes our criterion in a dynamic way rather than "good" in a static sense.

The anthem is not to be discarded, of course, but it is clearly secondary in liturgical importance to congregational song, and when the people can sing, it is preferable that they do so. There are times and occasions when an anthem is needed for something the people cannot do. All too often the anthem has been stuck into worship without any clear(idea of its liturgical) function or purpose. In such cases the liturgical action grinds to a halt, and the anthem becomes a musical interlude or even entertainment. At best, an anthem can function as an integral part of the service of the Word, acting as a commentary and interpretation on one or more of the lessons. In this role (as a gradual between lessons), the anthem can be music difficult or impossible for the congregation. This means that the musician must take seriously the cycle of time in the church year and that the anthem is chosen because it is liturgically appropriate, not just because it is beautiful. Fortunately, it often can be both. It also means that when the congregation itself can sing suitable music, there is no need for an anthem.

The most important function of a choir has often been the most neglected. We speak of training and undergirding congregational singing.(One of the chief jobs of a choir is to make itself unnecessary,) but there is little likelihood this will happen at the rate music changes. Most of us are cowards when it comes to singing new and unfamiliar music. Choir members explore, practice, and become familiar with new music. They can undergird the singing of new music so that their role becomes that of risk takers, as teachers should be.

Some of the most creative uses of choirs in recent times have been where choir members have infiltrated the congregation and helped people sing by simply doing it well themselves. When we think of all the time and money spent on choir robes, choir processions, and choir stalls, it seems a pity we have been so slow in realizing that choirs exist, above all else, to help everyone exercise his priestly ministry in common worship. Like incense, a choir may make its contribution by losing itself. Even when together, choirs ought to be located where they are visibly a part of the congregation and (not a separate body.) The acoustics of the building will help dictate the choir's location. But we desperately need the choir to help us sing old music better and to "sing a new song."

In short, we need church musicians far more than ever before, but their role is changing drastically from primarily that of performers to include that of enablers. The glorification of God is accomplished by the sanctification of man. Singers glorify God best by helping the congregation offer their praise. Even an amateur sport needs professionals to coach the players and to help them develop their own skills even further. And we are more interested in playing the game than in winning aesthetic laurels, though it is desirable to do both.

I

We have seen a great widening in the horizons of church music in the last few years. Much of the change has been sparked by the Roman Catholic Church with its resolution to give the mass back to the people. Catholic congregations had little invested in hymnbooks full of old hymns. They had few, if any, old favorites to unlearn. And so they could begin with the present. For five years now their presses have produced numerous booklets of new hymns and service music. One of the best of these paperback hymnals is the ecumenical version of the *Hymnal for Young Christians.*[2] Similar booklets appear

[2] (22 East Huron Street, Chicago 60611: F.E.L. Church Publications, 1968).

almost monthly. A good Protestant contribution is Carlton R. Young's *Songbook for Saints and Sinners.*[8]

This bothers some people because music takes time to learn, and therefore they hate to abandon it. It is certainly safe to say that much new church music will not endure. But why should permanence be a requisite of church music? A sermon is a disposable art form and most people are just as glad. Much of the new church music that is relevant today definitely will not endure. After all, probably ninety percent of the church music of any age has disappeared and no one misses it. Charles Wesley wrote over six thousand hymns, many were set to music, and today we sing less than a hundred of them. We might sing far fewer had they not been winnowed out of so large a pile. The impermanency of much recent church music is not necessarily to its discredit. It may be its strength.

In an age where everything else seems to be undergoing rapid change, church music may need to be in flux even more than it is at present. Just because some tunes and texts have been preserved so well in hardbound hymnals does not make them honest, sincere, and relevant today. Hymnody is not something to be preserved throughout time, like the gospel, but a form through which the gospel is conveyed. The gospel fits into many containers but never can be confused with any of them. Of the new church music some bits may well endure. (Peter Scholtes' "They'll Know We Are Christians by Our Love" is one of our candidates.) But most of the rest can and ought to slip away, unnoticed and unmourned except by those who collect royalties.

Most of the new church music follows the popular musical idioms of our time—country, western, folk song, blues, rock, and so on. Some of this music, of course, has been more than remotely inspired by very "square" styles: baroque and even Gregorian chant. Part of the appeal of the newer music is that it is already familiar. Much of this music, though not all, has a strong rhythm that pulls the body into the act. Older people still remember when this was true of church music until they were taught to be ashamed of it. Much of the new music is also readily singable.

[8] (5707 West Corcoran Place, Chicago 60644: Agape, 1971).

In terms of musical craftsmanship, much of this music is inferior. The melodies are often banal, the rhythms crude, and the harmony repetitious. So what? Its lack of complexity and sophistication may be an asset. Grandmother Moses knew nothing about painting. But she painted. Everyone can sing the new church music because he is already familiar with the same rhythms if he lives anywhere near a radio, phonograph, or television set. And they are rather hard to avoid today. Much of the newer music may be good for the praise of God in our here and now because its forms are often natural for us. Finding what is natural and, possibly, enduring will entail considerable trial-and-error probing.

The texts are another concern in song. We have finally weaned some of our people away from what were called "gospel songs" but usually were anything but gospel since they talked mostly about how (we felt about Jesus rather than what God had done in Christ for us.) The hymnal texts of the eighteenth century and the office hymns translated in the nineteenth century were a real liberation from the subjectivity of the gospel song. But this is no longer our only alternative. Some of the new hymn texts are both more biblical and relevant than anything else now available. W. F. Jabusch's "Whatsoever You Do" is simply a paraphrase of Matthew 25:31-46 but done in a way inescapably relevant today. Some of these biblical passages have not spoken in the same way to past ages and may not to future ones. Even the missionary hymns of a couple of generations ago now seem strangely foreign and imperialistic to us. They were once relevant and apt, but we have changed. Kipling has disappeared from hymnals, and "From Greenland's Icy Mountains" now fly American bombers.

Indeed, if we were honest, we could not sing the words of many hymns found in our hymnals with fervor. Take away the music and the words would often disturb us. There are plenty of exceptions and some of the oldest ones are still fresh. "O For a Thousand Tongues to Sing" or "O God, Our Help in Ages Past" may outlast many others. Many of us cannot sing with sincerity about our conversion day or in graphic descriptions of the life hereafter. We can and want to sing about the love of Christ here and now. Too much of our diet of hymns has been pablum or indigestible. A much greater honesty is needed and is provided in many of the new hymns.

It seems very likely that the days of the bound hymnbook will soon end. People want to sing, but they want to sing in ways natural to their times and in words akin to their sincere belief. The new music tries to do this, succeeds frequently, fails often, (but at least makes the effort) Looseleaf and paperback hymnbooks can fill the gap. We can afford to burn them every five years or more often. (A new song, sung with enthusiasm and conviction, is a fuller expression of our worship than an old song, sung without either.) After all, there is no Christian music. All we have are sounds that we use to express Christian faith the best we can in any age.

As often happens, sometimes a big step forward is the result of a long leap backward. The psalms have always been the greatest hymnbook of the church. They have been sung in translation in Christian worship since the second century, and in metrical paraphrases in the vernacular from the sixteenth century on. But often putting the psalms into metrical paraphrases involved a more ingenious than faithful rendering. A French priest, Father Joseph Gelineau, has developed a method of singing the psalms that combines the best of professional and amateur music while using the good translations of the texts.[4] An ideal way to use these is with individual singers scattered through the congregation. Since the verses are of varying lengths, they are all sung by soloists. A woman soloist behind may sing one verse, a man up front another, and we never know from whom or where the next verse will come. At the beginning and at the end of each verse a refrain (antiphon) is sung by the entire congregation. Gelineau's setting of Psalm 23 (Roman Catholic 22) is particularly effective. Another possibility is to have the verses sung chorally or simply spoken by a reader. The Gelineau psalmody allows us to use the psalms as written without mangling each verse to fit a metrical pattern. It also combines both trained solo and congregational singing. They certainly are compatible.

Much of what we have said about congregational and choral

[4] Published in various editions by Gregorian Institute of America, 2115 W. 63rd St., Chicago 60636. Inexpensive editions for congregational use are available in leaflet form.

music also applies to instrumental music. The literature for the pipe organ was brought to such perfection in the eighteenth century that we have never gotten over it. As George Bernard Shaw remarked, Shakespeare's greatness had ruined English drama (until Shaw). There is nothing wrong with the pipe organ (though plenty with imitations of it). The only problem is that it is not the only possibility. However excellent and versaltile it may be, it still is basically only one sound. Why in the modern musical world limit ourselves to a diet of nothing but steak when we could also have salads, vegetables, and dessert?

There is nothing more Christian about the pipe organ than any other instrument. Indeed in the East it was barred from churches for associating with taverns, as we might exclude the juke box. Maybe the guitar has already been overused. At least it ought not make us forget the other string instruments, to say nothing of the horns, woodwinds, and percussion. The horns are particularly useful for processions.

The guitar has been popular in churches in recent years because so many people play it. But we ought also to point out the advantages of instrumental music other than the organ. Guitars require very little investment, if any, on the part of the congregation. Many people can share in playing them and they can play almost anywhere in the building. If we are willing to have volunteer singers in the choir, we can tolerate volunteer instrumentalists too. They will give us more variety and possibilities than we have ever experienced in the past.

Of course, music is only a small part of our world of sound. Most life is pure noise, that is, unorganized sound. A composer takes noise and organizes it on a vertical structure (harmony) and on a horizontal one (melody). But life, we know, is not that way. It is noise, random noise without much order and coherence. Music is a very small part of the sound of life. Most life is noise without sense and structure. Music is a very limited range of noise. Can we go beyond music in our use of noise for worship?

Noises are much more a part of worship than we usually realize. The shuffling of feet, the turning of pages, the fuss of children, books being pulled out and put away, the sputter of radiators, assorted coughs and sneezes, all are a part of being a group of humans at worship. And we can hardly avoid in the city sounds from outside—traffic, airplanes, and sirens. Even Quaker worship cannot be altogether silent with people present. We learn to hear just those noises we want to and ignore the rest. If our eyes were shut we would hear much that we now tune out.

But sometimes the noises of humanity can be deliberately used in worship. Modern technology makes it possible for us to go beyond music as it has traditionally been scored for instruments or voice and bring any sound into worship. Such noises can be collected on tape and used when desired. Sounds of pain and suffering, sounds of joy and rapture, sounds of all types and conditions of people, these may become part of our intercessions for God's creatures. On special occasions a whole "inventory of effects" may prompt our recalling and responding to God. Such sounds can be used at random or organized. They may help us to realize the presence of God in all life and our need in all things to glorify God.

It is exciting to live in an age when we can hear sounds never heard before by men. Whereas we have mentioned collected sound, there is also the possibility of creating entirely new sounds by various electronic devices, such as the Moog synthesizer. Electronic music is being increasingly used in television and movies and some has been used in worship. There is no reason why it cannot be used in the place of other instrumental music in churches. Some, such as Richard Felciano's anthem "Pentecost," can be used in combination with human voices. We are just beginning to see the possibilities that electronic music offers in adding a whole new gamut of sound to our worship.

Some have spoken of music as simply a way of communicating information. It should not surprise us, then, that church music has varied in every time. Each age has different aspects of reality that it learns to voice. We should rejoice that we have found new tongues with which to sing our "new song to the Lord." We can be confident that "a people yet unborn shall praise the Lord" with still newer forms of which we have not yet dreamed.

If sound is a crucial part of Christian worship in the modern world, then that which is seen comes close in importance. Once again, the contemporary changes in communications are making a profound impact on worship. Preliterate man found most of the communication in the medieval mass to be visual. Postliterate man may someday do the same. We are bombarded by so many hours of television that we already depend on visual modes of communication for much of the information we need.

We can already trace some of the effects of this visual stimulation on the things we do and like. Researches have shown that the advent of television has stimulated our interest in texture. Since touching is so closely related to seeing, this is not strange. Architecture seems to have become more serious about texture, and we see many recent buildings that are a pleasure to touch. The move seems away from sleek glass and steel buildings to rough-textured surfaces whether in wood, brick, or large-aggregate concrete. One can recognize the same concern for texture in the sudden popularity of banners in churches. Textiles fascinate because of their texture as much as for their color and shapes.

The advent of color television has emphasized another dimension of perception. We are much more color conscious. Look at what has happened to men's clothing since the advent of color television. Once only a tie added color to a white shirt and grey flannel suit. Now the tie may be the most somber part of the ensemble. In our monochrome chapel we have moved from contentment with no color to painting the three movable liturgical centers in bright colors, underlining where the action centers. The colors, with shades carefully chosen by an architect for this particular building, are: font, blue; altar-table, red; and pulpit, yellow, green, and blue (emphasizing its form). Now we are becoming uneasy with monochrome classrooms. It took television to help us discover the rainbow.

We have spoken already of time as a form of communication and how the yearly cycle of time helps give meaning to our worship. And we have discussed how unchanging most of our church buildings remain throughout the year. Obviously

there is some need for constants. But that is all we have had
—the same building no matter what. There are times and
occasions when the building needs to communicate something
very specific: at funerals, weddings, Christmas, Easter, etc.
Various seasons of the church year have their own meanings
that the building ought to proclaim just as our clothing indicates the seasons of the weather. Much more ought to change
in the building than just the black and white numbers on the
hymnboard.

Though we cannot have a whole new building each time
(yet), the same space, by making visual changes, can be altered
dramatically from time to time. We know how drastically a
new piece of furniture or painting can change the whole context of a living room. The same is true with churches. We
can have a different building when we need it—not every
Sunday but every time an event of special meaning to the
community's life comes around. Bits of visual art make the
difference. All it takes is that most priceless object, imagination, plus some work. Not much money, not much effort, but
a tremendous reliance on trained imagination is required.

It is time to stop thinking of art as something precious that
must be preserved but as something all around us if we but
have eyes to see it. Some people have the gift of seeing the
beautiful and meaningful all around us and we call them artists. But most people have never really learned to see. The
artist can take ordinary objects and make them reveal part of
the gospel. Much new religious art is disposable, like sermons.
Unfortunately it is as hard to get people to throw away banners
after they have been used as it is to get preachers to discard
old sermon manuscripts.[5] Permanency is not so good a criterion
of church art today as is adequacy. Mass produced goods are
not the answer. The visual arts ought to reflect the life and
faith of a specific people who use them on a particular occasion. One is reminded of the Swiss sculptor, Jean Tinguely,
who built a piece of sculpture that was designed to destroy
itself. It succeeded. Many new visual arts are for the here and

[5] Cf. Reinhold Marxhausen's *Please Dispose After Use: Disposable Forms
for Worship* (Youth Ministry Materials, P.O. Box 14325, St. Louis, Mo.
63178).

now and, as so much else in our society, are disposable after use.

Our goal, then, is not permanency but aptness for the time, place, and people. Again, we are talking in terms of "good for," i.e., art that will vary according to people and conditions in helping us approach reality at a deeper level, receive insight into the ways of God, and make our responses. The same criterion of fitness might be applied to sermons. But, of course, visual arts are not sermons. Where a sermon is apt to be explicit and highly defined, the visual arts use a different approach. They usually are not explicit. Often they are susceptible to several layers of interpretation and feature an ambiguity sermons rarely tolerate. It is important to remember that visual arts are not sermons any more than sermons are visual arts.

Protestantism, though welcoming music from the first, has been slow in taking seriously the visual arts in worship. This is not because the Reformers did not take art seriously. Maybe they took it too seriously. They had a great deal of respect for the power of the arts to lead people astray by confusing the ultimate with the proximate. Religious art made the divine too near at a time when the Reformers, particularly the Calvinists, wanted instead to emphasize the utter transcendence of God. The Reformers had so much respect for the potency of religious art that they could not tolerate it as harmless. So they were compelled to destroy it. Art could not be allowed to destroy truth.

We, instead, simply shipped it off to museums where liturgical art was framed between nudes and landscapes. We admired it but we did not respect it for its power to bring the divine closer. When we finally did admit religious art back into churches in the nineteenth century, it was totally powerless. Things looked just the way they did to a camera only a little sweeter, a little more saccharine. Art had lost its mystery and was used to illustrate rather than to probe. Such art revealed nothing to us, for it showed us only what we could already see. It had no power. And so it exchanged substance for sentimentality, emphasizing the obvious. When the salt lost its taste, we seasoned with sugar instead. One of the dangers in disposable arts is that often they do not go much beyond the obvious, making only minimal demands on us.

The more permanent visual arts will not let us off so easily any more. They have a potency to communicate something beyond themselves. We do not come up against something that reflects us but something that makes us look deep inside ourselves. Sometimes we wonder, not what do I think of this head of Christ but what does it think of me? We do not have the fear of liturgical art that the Reformers had because they were afraid of an idolatry of objects. We are more fearful of an idolatry of self, and liturgical art may be our protection from that. The visual arts, today, may point us to the transcendent that the Reformers sought to safeguard.

III

We turn now to examine actual practice in the use of new forms of the visual arts. This does not mean we would exclude the traditional art forms—painting, murals, sculpture, and stained glass—but presumes that such may be present and that we want to venture into less familiar areas of visual stimulation. The arts that we shall discuss here are better seen in place in churches than described. But since we are limited to the printed page, we shall have to tell rather than show.

When we made a banner for All Saints' Day in 1966, we were not aware of any churches in this area using banners. But since then most of the Methodist, Presbyterian, Episcopalian, and Disciples of Christ churches have. In five years they have become common. We are not talking about something any longer foreign to the experience of many Christians in all parts of the country. In the recent past, textile arts in the churches were largely confined to hangings on pulpits, lecterns, and altar-tables. These were usually of shiny silky fabrics with timid conventional symbols in gold. Episcopalians and Lutherans might go a step further and use colored vestments, but rarely did these become venturesome in design or material. Today the designs and types of textile arts in use are almost unlimited.

It is interesting to note this quick welcome that textile arts have received in Protestant churches. Much of this is due, no doubt, to their impermanency. One of the best things about banners is that one can get rid of them. Textiles do not look permanent and so do not threaten anyone. We know they will be gone in time. Even the Pentecost season does not last forever, and only pulpit and lectern hangings would normally be left up throughout a long season. The observance of octaves (eight-day commemorations) makes good sense for many textiles.

There are other reasons for the appeal of textile arts, especially banners. Textures, especially rough textures, stimulate the sense of touch. This is very true of sculpture. We feel them with our eyes. When we take little children to the store we say: "Now, see with your eyes only." But they know better because humanity wants to touch things. We learn to do this with our eyes. But people come up to a banner saying, "I want to see that," and they reach out and touch it. Textiles also have movement. They ought to be hung so they can move freely. Some can be suspended from a fish-hook swivel so they revolve even with a slight breeze from moving people. These banners can be the same on both sides (as in see-through banners), different on either side, or cylindrical. Three dimensional banners are quite possible.

Banners can be made of almost anything that will hang. Burlap is frequently used, perhaps too frequently. It comes in many colors, has a strong texture, and is cheap. Felt is popular because of colors, the ease in glueing things on it, and the lack of danger of raveling. Almost any cloth, especially prints, stripes, and plaids, may form the background. We are not limited to cloth. Aluminum foil may be used behind other materials such as net (in various layers and colors). Wrinkles make it faceted. Oil cloth, vinyl, newspaper clippings, canvas, upholstery and drapery materials, and corduroy have been used. The possibilities of color, texture, and shape are as wide as one's imagination.

Banners need not be elaborate. In one small town church, an artist prepared a banner to reinforce the sermon each Sunday.[6] They were extremely effective—and discarded each

[6] A number of exciting banners and other art forms may be studied by renting (for a nominal fee) a slide-tape lecture on liturgical arts by Professor Reinhold Marxhausen of Concordia College, Seward, Nebraska. His filmstrip, "Seeing Is Believing," is an excellent introduction to this whole area: Geo. A. Pflaum, Publishers, 38 West Fifth Street, Dayton, Ohio 45402.

week. One of the key needs in banners (and all art forms) is knowing when to stop. In some cases pure color alone says more than an elaborate design. Many congregations spend considerable money each Easter for flowers to express the joy and hope of the resurrection. We found that we could string twelve dollars' worth of colored broadcloth across the width of the nave from the pillars on each side. Several were slit halfway down the middle so that the "Y" form made a hand gesture of shouting for joy. The effect was far greater than hundreds of dollars' worth of flowers—and we still have the cloth. At Pentecost or ordinations, long pieces of red cloth can be suspended in random lengths from the ceiling. An arrow-like point may be cut in the end or not. This may be far more effective than making banners with words ("Come Holy Spirit") or symbols (tongues of flame) and far easier. Knowing when to stop is hardest of all but vital.

Many banners contain verbal texts, particularly fragments from the liturgy or Scriptures. One, for Lent, said "Father forgive" beneath a cross torn from newspaper headlines. Others take antiphons from the psalms or introits. But there is a temptation to use too many words so that the banner is explicit and viewers bring little to it. Banners are not a print medium. Their message depends on the viewer and they must be terse and provocative. Professor Marxhausen uses secular slogans which gain their impact from the context of a church setting, e.g., "When you care enough to send the very best" at Christmas. We used "hour after hour" and a cross during Lent. Good banners make people wrestle out their own meaning. The creation story is caught in "Good! Good! Good!" for those biblically literate. "Here Now," with a crude letter "X" marking the spot, pulls in several layers of meaning, especially at the Lord's Supper.

Humor is serious too. A student showed up at an Ascension Day service with a banner saying, "By God, He made it." When you turn that over you find the prologue to the Fourth Gospel condensed into five words. A nun showed up in a procession where other nuns were carrying the usual "Love" banners but hers said "Do it, dammit." There is a wide range of possibilities in verbal texts if they make us probe beneath the immediate.

Words ought not be used if you can say it any other way. Banners can be pictorial, using recognizable objects that can be identified by their shape. Stars, mangers, and people are examples. Here again there is no point in showing the obvious. An Easter banner made on see-through mesh featured eighty butterflies cut from different kinds of dress materials. A simple shape like an arrow poses all kinds of possibilities, such as a white arrow descending in Advent (maybe against a purple background to a black globe), arrows pointing four directions in Epiphany (maybe overlying the same globe), a strong upward arrow at Easter (and Ascension), and then a red arrow coming down at Pentecost. Study traffic signs and see how they are moving to more images and fewer words (as happened long ago in multilingual Europe).

Then there are more abstract possibilities which demand greater degrees of wrestling. Three disks of shades decreasing in intensity, strong vertical stripes in the weave of the material, and chiffon overlays pointing upward made an Easter banner. Empty bread wrappers arranged in a random pattern created a communion banner. A good exercise is to say "Lift up your hearts" without using words.

Banners ought always be designed by someone experienced in textiles. They should not be confused with painting because the possibilities and limitations are utterly different. Banners must be clear from a hundred feet distance and few paintings are meant to be. Details such as facial features are impossible. We work instead with color, shape, and texture, and these should not be confused with shading, lines, and fine detailing which can be done in other arts.

Negative space, the areas not covered with anything, are just as important as those covered. Sometimes these spaces can be transparent (mesh, or chiffon, plastics) or several layers built on one another. But they are a part of the design and of what it communicates and not just background. Sometimes they may reflect the liturgical season by their color and texture.

Generally the best way to begin is by having the artist make a sketch and then a full-size cartoon, cutting out pieces from this. He then chooses swatches of cloth for each piece. Anyone who can sew can then make the banner, though it is wise to have the artist around so he can play around with it until things come right. The sewing can be of all types. Appliqué is common and some glue materials on felt though they are apt to come loose with movement. Couching is often used. Embroidery can be done though it does not show up from much distance. Borders may involve a pattern cut into material itself (such as felt), threads pulled from a woven material to make a fringe, or a braid added.[7]

There are many possibilities for textile art in the conventional forms of hangings from pulpits and lecterns. These are, in effect, small banners though usually retained for longer. It has become rather common in recent years to avoid altar-table hangings in favor of a simple linen runner that makes the altar-table more of a table than a monument. The same may be becoming true in the case of the pulpit. We have already mentioned the wide possibilities vestments offer.

One of the delights in textile arts is that many people of the congregation, including shut-ins who cannot serve in other ways, can take part in the creation of banners, hangings, and vestments. Frequently the result, if well designed, is far better than the safe mediocrity of the commercial suppliers. Certainly it will be cheaper. But the greatest benefit of all may be the sense of giving that those who have shared in making it will feel, and the sense that they are offering worship just as much as those who give of their time and talents in the choir. We involve many people in a variety of ways in planning and preparing for worship today.

Other media we are taking more seriously are the graphic arts. These may take many forms. Church bulletin boards have abounded with posters for years, but very few of these would we call art or care to have inside the church proper. This is changing both within churches and outside. Good poster art is becoming more common, and some cities even have stores that sell nothing but posters. Some of these posters are explicitly religious and many in a subtle way.

[7] Cf. *Banners, Banners, Banners, Etc.,* by Robert W. Andersen and Richard R. Caemmerer, Jr. (1801 West Greenleaf Ave., Chicago 60626: Christian Art Associates, 1967); *Banners and Hangings,* by Norman LaLiberté and Sterling McIlhaney (New York: Reinhold Publishing Co. [Van Nostrand-Reinhold Books], 1966).

Others may be ordered from firms specializing in religious posters.[8] One of these firms inquires, if a picture is worth ten thousand words, how many sermons is a good poster worth? It is not just a sales pitch. One sometimes remembers a poster or banner longer than a sermon. Some of these posters can be used inside a church and, since they are cheap, they need only be used once or twice.

On occasion members of the congregation may make posters to be used in worship. Sometimes even graffiti scratched on long rolls of butcher paper may be used. At a service of Christian unity these had scrawled on them, in a variety of styles and hands, the word and number "one." Frequently photographs can be used, especially when blown up to large dimensions. This can be done commercially at relatively small cost. Often the juxtaposition of a contemporary photograph and a scriptural text: "Feed my sheep" or "When was it that we saw you?" makes an unforgettable impact.

The first thing that happens when we enter most churches is that someone puts a bulletin into our hands. It gives us a fairly important impression of what the service is going to be before a single word is spoken. All too often, the bulletin is a poorly mimeographed job on cheap paper featuring some sentimental art. How many times have the Grand Canyon, a New England village, candles, chalices, and Christmas trees appeared on bulletins? To say nothing of the church's name and address though we are already there. It makes a sensitive person want to turn and run. A picture of the church's exterior is not much better since we may have come inside to escape just that.

How much better is it to be handed something that portrays a basic Christian concept, especially one revolving around the lessons for that particular Sunday in the church's life! These are available through several bulletin services, some of them consistently good, others having their better weeks.[9]

[8] Argus Communications, 3505 North Ashland Avenue, Chicago 60657: Liturgical Press, Collegeville, Minnesota 56321; Abbey Press, Saint Meinrad, Indiana 47577; Corita, Inc., 5126 Vineland, North Hollywood, California 91601; Geo. A. Pflaum, Publishers, 38 West Fifth Street, Dayton, Ohio 45402. Most of these presses publish catalogs.

[9] Biblical and social concerns are often expressed well by the United Church Press series (1507 Race St., Philadelphia, 19102). Sacred Design

There is another possibility, that of members of the congregation creating their own bulletins and having them printed by offset printing. When the costs of paper and labor expended in cutting, correcting, and running a stencil is figured, the expenses may be comparable. With offset printing, one can include anything in the bulletin that can be pasted in and has good contrasts. Permissions will be necessary to reproduce copyrighted materials. Music, typewritten material, woodcuts, and sketches by pencil, ball-point pen, or magic marker will reproduce well. Photographs require a prescreened print which can be made at additional cost. Colored paper may cost no more and colored print will cost one run for each additional color. If there is talent to design bulletins in a congregation, it may well be worth the effort to create them locally rather than buying the commercial type. Art instructors who specialize in graphics may rejoice in having this a project for their students. Most towns of any size will have several firms that do offset printing.

There are other art forms that we have every reason to utilize. Members of many congregations have some skill in ceramics and can make short candlesticks for the altar-table and might even attempt chalices. A stand for a paschal candle (large candle for the Easter season representing Christ as not extinguished by death) can be made of ceramics. Ours suggests a pile of blossoms, each opening upward toward the light. College art departments often have people teaching metalwork who may be willing to design and make metal chalices. If we shop around a bit, we can find beautiful decanters for communion wine at Danish import stores and attractive baskets for bread and offertory plates sell very cheaply as oriental imports. Maybe we shall someday see the end of brass church goods.

There are countless ways in which a variety of art forms can be used in the church. The most priceless ingredient is imagination. With imagination, the simple and ready-at-hand can be made to bloom and become a part of the work of

---

(840 Colorado Avenue, South, Minneapolis 55416) and Anchor Church Suppliers, Inc. (3810 West Broadway, Minneapolis 55422) offer a wide choice plus subscription service. Liturgical Press (Collegeville, Minn. 56321) offers a Catholic subscription series better than the slick and obvious.

proclaiming the gospel. Without imagination, you end up going to the church goods store and paying a great deal more for less. We have put the musicians to work praising God. Why do we not also turn to his praise the hands of the artists who may be as numerous in many churches as musicians?

The day has arrived when we can go beyond art as something present and use electronic means for presenting things absent. We can now see anything in the world and create sights and combinations of sights that exist only momentarily. Slides, filmstrips, and movies give us the possibility of showing anything the external eye can see. By the use of colors or oil and water combinations in an overhead projector, it is possible to present abstract scenes never before or never again seen.

The juxtaposition of several images produces all kinds of possibilities. If we project together slides of the Statue of Liberty and the Golden Gate Bridge, we suggest America as geography. But if we replace the Bridge with a slide of Red Square, Moscow, we call attention to two contrasting social and economic systems. We can project simultaneously several images on a large scrim, screen, or shower curtain (for rear view projections). Whether done apparently at random or deliberately organized, relationships—both temporal and spatial—create their own meanings.

Motion pictures present other opportunities and challenges. Since they involve both sound and sight, adequate equipment and light control are necessary. Unless there is print on the film, one can project from behind a scrim. Numerous short films, some based on psalms and other scriptural passages, are available.[10] We must be careful that they do not submerge the rest of the service.

But these are dangerous and tempting grounds. The power of the electronically produced visual images is so strong that we must know what we are doing. These media can dominate everything else so easily that the rest of the service seems

[10] Many excellent five-minute films on the psalms may be rented cheaply from Father Peyton's Family Theater Productions, 7201 Sunset Boulevard, Hollywood, California 90046. They may be interspersed with the psalms sung by the Gelineau method.

overwhelmed. If we try film to illustrate the sermon, we may find we have to stop preaching. It may be a blessing that few churches (as of now) have unbroken hard surfaces on which images may be projected or natural lighting can be controlled.

We can close with a brief commentary on a special service. We called it our "Joyful Noise" service. It was the Lord's Supper, and the theme we were trying to stress was the presence of God in all life and the need to take all things God has created with thanksgiving (I Timothy 4:4). The situation was a group of seminarians, thoroughly familiar with the communion service, and a building where shutters give considerable control over natural light.

In essence, the "Joyful Noise" service was an overlay of three items: the communion service exactly as normally performed, a continuous series of collected noises, and random slides changing automatically at eight-second intervals. The effect was to pull people into the service because they were constantly forced to make their own associations among the three items that were in process—Lord's Supper, sounds, and sights. The noises began with a jet airplane taking off but from that point on they were completely random—a crowd at a football game, a rooster crowing, a baby crying, a ping-pong ball game, traffic, sea gulls, an ambulance, a train passing, etc. We taped these sounds from sound records but one can easily collect sounds with a portable tape recorder. Someone controlled the volume so that it did not drown out those parts of the service spoken by individuals or the sermon. The slides were meant to appear in a random series though a great deal of time had gone into their selection and sequence. A random sequence often takes much more time to prepare than a recognizable scheme. The slides included people, civic buildings, a funeral, children playing, paintings (a few of religious subjects), and landscapes.

People responded well by being forced to work hard to put together these sights and sounds with God's gift of himself to us in the Lord's Supper. For several people, mental barriers between the sacred and secular were erased. The sermon made this intent explicit. Probably that was unnecessary. At any rate, many were amazed at the high degree of effort they had exerted throughout the service. Such a service would not be repeated often, if for no other reason because of the tremendous amount of preparation it requires. It does illustrate well the power relatively unsophisticated techniques and equipment can have in helping us worship God.

We now have available a fantastic array of possibilities in using sounds and sights to worship God. If the art forms become simply toys that we enjoy playing with, they can be demonic and destructive. And it is very likely that this is what will happen if we do not think through the pastoral, theological, and historical norms of Christian worship. But if we have done this necessary work, we may be able to use these new forms in constructive ways, so that all our senses can get into the act and praise their Creator.

VII

SACRAMENTS AS SIGN-ACTIVITIES

It has become common in recent years to talk about multi-media worship as if that were something new and exciting. The Christian sacraments have always been multi-media worship. Indeed, this is their most distinctive feature. Throughout history, much of the controversy about the sacraments has revolved around the use of matter—e.g., the cup to the laity—as well as the form and proper ministrant. The sacraments involve a variety of media that stimulate, at one time or another, all our senses.

We often fail to grasp this aspect of the sacraments because we bury them under a haystack of words, emphasizing only one medium, the spoken word. As a result, frequently the sacraments become a mere appendage to the service of the Word. Their distinct qualities as vehicles of meaning are hid. The Protestant emphasis on verbal communication has distorted the sacraments so that they are underacted and over-articulated.

John Calvin knew better when he spoke of the sacraments as special means in which God "so tempers himself to our capacity that . . . he condescends to lead us to himself even by these earthly elements, and to set before us in the flesh a mirror of spiritual blessings." [1] Man does not live on a diet of words alone but has to be shown as well as told. Calvin insists on the need of signs of God's love even for the elect.

[1] *Institutes of the Christian Religion* IV, xiv, 3, ed. by John T. McNeill and trans. by Ford Lewis Battles (Philadelphia: Westminster Press, 1967), II: 1278.

"Because we have souls engrafted in bodies, he [God] imparts spiritual things under visible ones."[2] The sacraments reflect man's capacity to perceive God's love.

In recent years theologians have moved to a more anthropological approach to the sacraments, underlining Calvin's words just cited. They have rediscovered that "the sacraments are first and foremost symbolic acts or activity as signs" and not just abstract theological problems about grace.[3] Since both Reformers and Tridentine Catholics agreed on the function of the sacraments as signs, this vital aspect tended to be overlooked in favor of the controversial issues in the sixteenth century and since. Much effort has been expended in wrangling about the nature of the "inward and spiritual grace given" in the sacraments with hardly a second look at the "outward and visible sign."

It was in effect, though never consciously so, a dualistic approach as if "outward and visible" could be ignored in favor of the "inward and spiritual," as if man lived in two separate and distinct compartments. Theologians let liturgists worry about the shape of the liturgy and these, in turn, occupied themselves with historical studies, never venturing close to anthropology. In the modern world, such divisions seem absurd. It now appears that the theological controversies of the Reformation and since have often neglected some of the most obvious aspects of the sacraments. The history of doctrine might have been considerably different if all disputants had focused more on the sacraments as signs.

We can take an example from the modern world to show how closely related the outward is to the inward. Automobiles are designed and sold not to demonstrate the achievements of engineers but of psychologists. An automobile sells because it embodies deep inward desires of power, mastery, the appearance of speed, and the opulence of wealth. Physically the automobile mirrors the human for whom it is intended, not the motor. All cars are alike in that they go the same speed (legally at least) and move us to the same places. But if a car model failed to make outward and visible that which is

[2] Ibid.
[3] E. Schillebeeckx, O.P., The Eucharist (New York: Sheed & Ward, 1968), p. 97.

inward in the purchaser, very few of that variety would be sold.

A new approach to the sacraments has developed in the past few years which tries to take into account the fullness of human perception. Some of this is indebted to philosophical studies on phenomenology, especially the writings of the agnostic French philosopher, Maurice Merleau-Ponty (1908-1961). His studies on perception have been used by theologians as a means to better understanding of signs and how they operate in communicating reality between people. This has led to a deeper exploration of the role of signs[4] in human life and especially of the sacraments in the life of Christians.

Signs are means by which men express interior realities to the world. Our physical bodies are signs of our existence to one another, our interiority made visible. Thus we use things as vehicles of meaning, and we can speak of reality itself existing within the sign. This becomes apparent when we see signs as ways people interact with one another. "The relationship between people comes into being in signs, and through signs it is further developed." [5] This appears in a kiss which becomes part of the relationship itself. "The kiss is love itself, embodied in a sign." In such a case, "the sign does not point to a reality outside itself; it is permeated with reality—with its own reality." [6] Of course signs can be false; Judas betrayed with a kiss. But this is abuse of a sign to deny what it expresses. A sign is expressive since "it must summon reality and make it present." Signs are vital parts of human relationships:

> Only through signs do we come to exist with and for one another. The relationship, in its search for signs, is searching for itself. No love exists that assumes no signs. A relationship can, of course, live on through signs from

[4] It should be clear that we are not relegating to the word "sign" the same meaning that Tillich gives it in *Dynamics of Faith* (New York: Harper & Row, 1957), pp. 41-42. The theologians we discuss here use it more nearly as Tillich (and others) use the word "symbol."

[5] Joseph Yperman, *Teaching the Eucharist* (New York: Paulist Press, 1968), p. 10.

[6] *Ibid.*, p. 11.

the past, at least for a time; but as time passes, the existence of the relationship is threatened.[7]

Many signs involve actions, and we have chosen to speak of a complex of several sign-acts as sign-activities. A good example is the giving of a wedding ring. On one level it is merely the exchange of a loop of gold. But that is to miss the reality of it altogether. "The concomitance of all these physical realities has only one basis, their real unity in the sign-act in which a man expresses the constancy of his love for a woman. If this is not real, nothing is."[8] We find the sign-activity of the wedding service a vital way of embodying a reality that exists between two persons. Words are only part of this particular sign-activity. In other cases words may be paramount or nonexistent.

It is difficult to find adequate sign-activities. That is why, when we find one that communicates well, we cling to it, using and reusing it. No matter how many sacraments we declare there to be, Protestants and Catholics cling to basically the same sign-activities for expressing the encounter of God and man. In the sacraments or sacramental acts, we have effective means of embodying the "divine bestowal of salvation in an outwardly perceptible form which makes the bestowal manifest; a bestowal of salvation in historical visibility."[9] Most Protestants would also argue that in preaching salvation is bestowed in audible form.

When incorporated into sign-activities, things become ways of expressing "meaning for" persons. This "meaning for" changes character as the relationship of persons and the sign vary:

A Greek temple is something different for its builders, for those who worship in it and for modern tourists. Man himself is essentially involved in this change of relationship, but it is not completely dependent on him—

---

[7] *Ibid.,* p. 12.
[8] Joseph M. Powers, S.J., *Eucharistic Theology* (New York: Herder and Herder, 1967), p. 167.
[9] E. Schillebeeckx, O.P., *Christ the Sacrament of the Encounter with God* (New York: Sheed & Ward, 1963), p. 15.

the *being* itself of things changes when the relationship is altered.[10]

What the temple signifies has become changed, so that its being as a sign is completely transformed though the stones remain unaltered. Another example is a gift of an article, perhaps of little or no value in itself. When a child picks a dead flower out of the wastebasket and gives it to us, it is a precious thing. Certainly its value no longer lies in its bloom and fragance—those are gone—but in the love expressed in the act of giving it to us. The giving of the object makes it full of meaning that is far more important than the object itself. Thus the act of giving the gift establishes or renews a relation between persons. In human relationships the use of sign-acts provides important vehicles of meaning.

Sign-acts cannot be purely arbitrary or accidental. The signification has to have either an obvious or commonly understood content. If it has to be explained to have meaning, it is a good indication it has little or none. If a person comes to the Lord's Supper as a nonbeliever, then he stands outside the relationship in which it has meaning and can hardly "discern the Body." To those within the relationship of faith, the sacraments do not seem arbitrary but part of the "promises" of Jesus Christ.

Yet even for the believer there is need for obviousness about what is intended by those sign-activities we call sacraments. Much of the intensity of meaning in any sign-act in encounters between people depends upon the clarity of the sign-act in representing what is intended. There is always danger of our actions being misunderstood unless we make our intentions clear by well-conceived actions or words. There is a similar need in the sacraments for real congruity between the whole sign-activity and that which it signifies. It is easy for practices and objects to become formalized and stylized so that any obvious relation between the sign-activity and what it signifies is lost. Catholics have sometimes found it takes more faith for children to believe that the wafers

[10] Schillebeeckx, *The Eucharist*, p. 113.

normally used at mass are really bread than it does to believe that the bread is Christ. There is precious little congruity between a tasteless wafer and real food. Theologically bread and the wafer may be the same, but anthropologically the sign value is drastically different. Our guiding principle in discussing the practical aspects of the sacraments will be to emphasize the congruity of the sign-activity and that which it signifies.

It is simply a matter of recognizing that signs depend upon human beings for meaning. We must approach the sacraments anthropologically as well as theologically. There is no less validity in a baptism performed with a teaspoonful of water than with a tub full. But as far as sign value is concerned, there is considerable difference. And since sign-activities depend upon recognition by people, baptism with a teaspoon is defective in all respects but the legalistic.

The sacraments, then, are sign-activities and reflect man's need to receive "spiritual things under visible ones." All the senses are part of the same act. If seeing is believing, so too is hearing, tasting, smelling, and touching. When we hide from ourselves just how sensuous the sacraments are, when we fail to take seriously the sign because we are only concerned about the inward, sign values are apt to suffer neglect. When we glimpse the unity of outward sign and inward grace, we are much more apt to take seriously our responsibilities for making the signs congruous.

No doubt the fullness of involvement in the sacraments accounts for their appeal to children. Any parent knows how difficult it is to keep a child quiet during a sermon. But the same child will stand on tiptoe to watch a baptism or the Lord's Supper. Once again, there is a good precedent for becoming like little children. Some congregations of youth have asked that the Lord's Supper be the normal Sunday service, whereas their parents have been heard to say that if you have it too often it will lose any meaning. The youth find meaning through action and involvement. The sacraments are more apt to provide this than other types of worship, at least when the sacraments' full power as sign-activities is taken seriously.

I

How, then, do we allow the sacraments their full sign values in our day? We shall look first at the practice of Christian initiation, then at the Lord's Supper. Much of what we have already said about physical movement also applies here.

We must begin by looking at that which we intend to signify by the sign-activities usually called baptism, confirmation, and first communion. We are not dealing with a simple, easily defined content but with a galaxy of metaphors. Initiation is a complex bundle of meanings reflected in a variety of sign-acts.

The best way of verbalizing these meanings of initiation is by recalling the biblical metaphors which we mentioned briefly in Chapter III. There are at least five key metaphors that the New Testament applies to baptism. The foremost of these is the sense of being united to Christ. This occurs in the act of being baptized into Christ's death and being raised with Christ (Romans 6:3; Colossians 2:12). Closely related is the concept of incorporation into the church and the sharing in the body of Christ (I Corinthians 12:13; Galatians 3:28). Other metaphors speak of our being born again (John 3:5) or regeneration (Titus 3:5) through baptism. Baptism involves the forgiveness of sins (Acts 2:38; 22:16) in which the act of washing is seen as that of cleansing of the conscience. Initiation is also connected with the reception of the Holy Spirit (Acts 2:38) or enlightenment (Hebrews 6:4). Other metaphors, less significant perhaps, include naming the name of the Lord, sealing, and ordination into the royal priesthood of the people of God.

The fascinating—and perplexing—problem of Christian initiation comes in keeping this whole galaxy in sight. If we were only trying to communicate one aspect, the work would be relatively simple. But the sacraments are multidimensional and like a precious stone owe much of their sparkle to their many facets. A single dimension might be easy to communicate but it would be a perversion of the meaning. To let go of one dimension is like dropping one side of the net and letting fish escape. One finds that there is always more depth to the sacraments than he has yet discovered. They are indeed a mystery whose bottom is not in sight. Fortunately the New Testament speaks of baptism in metaphors rather than in abstract definitions. "Buried with," "one body," "born over again," "wash away," "been enlightened" are all pictures of objects or actions. The New Testament uses visual images to interpret baptism. "Received the seal" or "laying on of the apostles' hands" are likewise action phrases that relate to confirmation. The history of initiation has been largely that of dramatizing the biblical metaphors.

How can these pictorial images be communicated through the actual practice of baptism, confirmation, and first communion? There are obvious differences between the practices of different denominations, especially between those that baptize infants and those that do not. But the problem of making these sign-activities congruous with what they signify is a common one, and many of the attempts to resolve this lead to similar practices.

The architectural setting of baptism is an important part of showing forth the meaning of this sacrament. In the later Middle Ages, it became customary to place the font at the entrance to parish churches, though earlier fonts had often been in a building or room separate from the church proper.[11] The admission into the church through baptism is still reflected in Catholic worship by having the rite begin with the candidates' entrance into the church building. Since the Reformation, the Reformed tradition, many Lutherans, and some Anglicans have placed the baptismal font near the pulpit and altar-table, so that baptism may be seen by the entire congregation. In recent years, some new Roman Catholic parishes have done likewise.

Which is the more effective sign, the font at the entrance to the church or in the midst of it? The church, after all, is people, not a building. To signify incorporation into the church by entering a church building may have some sign value, but to signify the same thing by bringing those to be baptized into the midst of the actual community of faith seems to be a more direct enactment of the meaning of this sacrament. The church building is only a shadow of the reality, the con-

---

[11] J. G. Davies, *The Architectural Setting of Baptism*, pp. 51-52.

gregation assembled is in fact the church. In some cases, the congregation can move and assemble about the font at the entrance.

There is another aspect to the location of the font or baptistery. Baptism is worship for us not only at the beginning of our Christian life but throughout it. Luther grasped this when he said of people:

> Their baptism should have been called to their minds again and again, and their faith constantly awakened and nourished. For just as the truth of this divine promise, once pronounced over us, continues until death, so our faith in it ought never to cease, but to be nourished and strengthened until death by the continual remembrance of this promise made to us in baptism.[12]

The baptismal font reminds us that we have been accepted by God and remain in his love. The font is a silent witness to God's loving acceptance of us and can remind us of this when visible to the whole congregation. In a few recent churches, the font has been placed near the main entrance to the church and yet remains visible to the whole congregation.

The size of the font testifies to the importance of baptism in the life of the congregation. Many fonts are only small basins, hardly much more than expensive candy dishes. Such fonts are inadequate for making Christian initiation an important sign-activity. What tiny fonts do portray, of course, is how casually and indifferently we have taken baptism. They are effective signs but of the wrong thing: of the neglect of baptism as a vital sign-activity in the life of the church. In several new Catholic churches in the Minneapolis area, the fonts are fully as large as the altar-table and leave no doubt that something important happens at baptism. The font cannot be neutral. It either proclaims loudly the importance of baptism or it underscores its neglect.

The design of the font is also a bearer of meaning. A font is basically a container for water, and yet many of them look

---

[12] "The Babylonian Captivity of the Church," *Luther's Works* (Philadelphia: Muhlenberg Press, 1959), XXXVI: 59.

like almost anything else. We achieved an appropriate shape in an inexpensive fashion by adopting a circular "flying saucer" sled that children in the North use for sliding. Painted silver and placed on a plywood stand, it is quite obvious that there is only one purpose in such a concave form—to hold water.

Baptism is to be seen, heard, and felt. If we speak in biblical terms of baptism as signifying the washing away and forgiveness of all that we have been—a divine nevertheless to our sin—then the sign value is greatly heightened if water splashes and drips so as to be seen and heard. This is hardly possible in a small font. Ideally the water container ought to be about two feet across in case we begin again to immerse babies. Skeptical people say nothing happens in baptism, and the way it is performed certainly reinforces this notion on several levels. When the water is never seen nor heard, the sign value of washing is tremendously diminished. It is not by accident that those denominations that do take baptism more seriously—Baptist, Disciples of Christ, Church of Christ—also make the water most apparent. Seeing and hearing the water also stimulates our sense of touch. The first step, then, in the reform of baptism is in making sure that we have an adequate font, suitably located.

In some situations it may be considered desirable to use various visuals when baptisms are held. Banners may be used which suggest water with biblical texts condensed such as: "We were baptized into Christ Jesus," "water of rebirth," "be born again," etc. Posters can be used for the same purpose. Some of the newer fonts have water flowing through them so that the sound of water may be heard throughout the baptismal service. Except in the Easter season, the paschal candle can be kept near the font and lighted during baptisms to stress our participation in the death and resurrection of Christ.

The mode of baptism is of great importance as far as making the sign-activity of this sacrament meaningful but of no consequence theologically. We often forget how late the practice survived of baptizing babies by immersing or dipping them. Though Calvin came to prefer pouring, both of Luther's baptismal liturgies specify the minister "shall take the child and dip [tauche=dunk] him in the font." [13] Luther preferred to "have those who are to be baptized completely immersed in the water . . . to give to a thing so perfect and complete a sign that is also complete and perfect." [14] The prayer books of the Church of England have all specified first dipping (if the child could "well endure" it) though it is likely that there have been few rubrics so consistently ignored (as John Wesley discovered to his dismay). The Roman Catholic Church had generally exchanged dipping for pouring by the end of the sixteenth century, though in the Archdiocese of Milan immersion survived.

New revisions point a return to dipping or immersing the child. The new Roman Catholic rite for infant baptism has the rubric: "He immerses the child or pours water upon it." [15] The proposed Episcopal rite is similar: "One of the ministers shall dip each candidate in the water or pour water on his head." [16] If the first (and preferable) form of these rubrics is followed, many existing fonts will have to be replaced by more ample ones.

Those who see for the first time baptism of adults by immersion are likely to be struck by the graphic nature of such baptism. There is an obvious and striking change in the person baptized. It is a telling moment of decision. Baptism as a descent into the waters dramatizes the sharing in Christ's death, burial, and resurrection in addition to acting out the washing from sin. Union to Christ and forgiveness are highlighted in immersion. Both apply to baptism of a baby by dipping.

If immersion is impossible, the next most expressive form of baptism is by pouring. The head of the infant is held over the font or the adult bows his head over it, and water is poured from a pitcher or shell over the top of the head. An

[13] J. D. C. Fisher, Christian Initiation: The Reformation Period (London: S.P.C.K., 1970), pp. 16 and 25.

[14] "Babylonian Captivity," Luther's Works, XXXVI: 68.

[15] Rite of Baptism for Children (Washington: United States Catholic Conference, 1969), p. 40. An excellent commentary on this rite appears in Robert Hovda's Manual of Celebration (Washington: The Liturgical Conference, 1970).

[16] Holy Baptism with the Laying-on-of-Hands (New York: Church Pension Fund, 1969), p. 39.

attractive ceramic pitcher may be used or, perhaps best of all, nature's own offering of a large scallop shell. Obviously the font must be large enough to catch the dripping water. This mode of baptism dramatizes the washing away of sin.

Last and least is a mode known as sprinkling in which a few drops of water in the minister's hand are placed on the top of the candidate's head. All too often it appears like a dry run and one wonders if the candidate ever gets more than a bit moist. The practice seems to have originated among the Reformed churches. John Knox's Genevan Liturgy of 1556 directs that the minister "taketh water in his hand and layeth it upon the childes forehead." [17] But even that sounds wetter than what often happens today. It is all too emblematic of our failure to use things and actions as significant sign-activities. Occasionally a rose bud is used to sprinkle and sentimentality fills the vacuum. Baptism was not instituted to help us simper in Christian cuteness but to proclaim what God does for us in Jesus Christ. A baptism is always an act of evangelism, proclaiming the good news of God's love. Sprinkling would hardly seem to project an adequate image of what God promises in baptism. The more graphic we make the act of washing, the greater is the sign value of the sacrament.

In baptism we are named in the name of the Trinity. When the child or adult is named ("John, I baptize you"), he is not given the human surname which he brings into this world, deriving from his earthly father (or occasionally mother), but the name of the Trinity. His Christian name is a "new name given us at our baptism, to remind us of our new birth." [18] It is also his name as a new member of the family of God and is repeated when he is confirmed, married ("I, John, take thee"), ordained, or buried. The naming of the child in the name of the Trinity ought to be heard clearly by all the congregation.

There are other parts of this sign-activity of baptism besides the central act of washing. One of the most important of these is the examination of those to be baptized or their

[17] William D. Maxwell, *The Liturgical Portions of the Genevan Service Book* (London: Faith Press, 1965), p. 111.

[18] Charles Wheatly, *A Rational Illustration of the Book of Common Prayer* (London: Henry G. Bohm, 1852), p. 346.

parents and sponsors. Usually questions and answers examine the intentions and hopes of those seeking baptism for themselves or those in their care. Another vital act is the profession of faith, either by those about to be baptized or by their parents and sponsors. From at least the third century this has taken the form we know as the Apostles' Creed, usually rendered in question form. These exchanges are verbal sign-acts and would seem best performed facing the congregation rather than the minister. Indeed, someone in the congregation could ask the questions of intention and faith. The kinetic act of washing complements the verbal profession of the creed. Baptism probably makes most sense at that point in the service where the creed normally occurs (often after the last lesson or after the sermon). Sometimes it will be preferable for the entire congregation to renew their affirmation of faith by joining those newly baptized in professing the creed.

Other actions have been a part of baptism since early times. Some of these would seem to have very little sign value at our point in American culture: blowing on the child, the giving of salt, exorcism, anointing with oil, the renunciation of Satan, and the Ephphetha (touching ears and mouth). It may be that there are places in the world today where these ceremonies still communicate and ought to be retained, but we would question their sign value in American culture.

But there are other sign-acts that may or may not help us visualize the significance of baptism. In this category we would put the invocation of the Holy Spirit upon the water (which the minister touches during this prayer), and making the sign of the cross on the forehead of the person baptized.

Two other actions would seem to have more definite sign value. Since people were baptized in the nude in the early church, having put off the garments and gold ornaments of the old Adam, a new white garment was placed on them immediately after baptism. Today, when babies are baptized by dipping, the same purpose is fulfilled by a white robe (the chrisom) placed over their shoulders or a white garment placed over the clothes of adults. It is at once a visualization of newness of life and a "token of innocency" acquired through putting on Jesus Christ. The new birth is made graphic in the person whose appearance is transformed by the new white robe which he wears throughout the rest of the service. In this instance, clothing can be a powerful mode of communication.

Another ancient practice is that of giving the newly baptized or his parents a candle lighted when possible from the paschal candle. It can be a sign of preparedness (the parable of the ten virgins, Matthew 25:1-13) or the enlightenment given by the Holy Spirit. Some may want to place these lighted candles at or on the altar-table when the baptism is ended. Candles have a character both festive and solemn (birthday and Christmas) that is quite appropriate to the birth of new members into the body of Christ.

There is much to be said for making Christian initiation a single act, especially for adults. It then moves directly from baptism to confirmation to first communion. Christianity has had trouble making up its mind about confirmation. The central act in Protestantism has been the laying on of hands which seem to be a more expressive (and biblical) act than a handshake. That which is represented here, of course, is the transmission of power from God, not just a friendly fellowship of like-minded Christians. Even that could be better shown by a kiss of peace in the form of an embrace of each person on whom hands have been laid.

The consummation of Christian initiation comes when those newly baptized and confirmed join the rest of the congregation at the Lord's table. In new white garments they stand out. Maybe they and their families ought to be honored guests, communicated first. They have been joined to the family of God like newly adopted children and hence join with the church in eating the Lord's Supper. Here incorporation into the church receives its most obvious expression. It is no accident that Communion is the only part of Christian initiation that is repeated.

Christian initiation, then, is an important sign-activity that expresses the whole gospel in short compass. Unfortunately we have not always realized the full evocative power of the various acts which it can include. Instead of being a brief formality, it is an important form of evangelism in witnessing to the love of God and strengthening the faith of the Christian community.

We find many of the same practical problems in allowing the Lord's Supper to express freely its fullness as a sign-activity. Like baptism, the Lord's Supper is based on a galaxy of biblical metaphors that often gets partially obscured. In this case, theological polemics have tended to polarize these as if the metaphors were alternatives instead of different facets of one and the same jewel. Champions of the commemorative aspects have been inclined to stand in opposition to those who stressed the reality of Christ's presence in the sacrament. Both were right and both were wrong, since each position needs to be complemented by the other.

Five biblical metaphors seem to stand out with regard to the Lord's Supper.[19] First of all is the joyful sense of thanksgiving, reflected in the accounts of the early Christians as they broke bread together with "glad and generous hearts" (Acts 2:46). The sense of joyful thanksgiving has been drastically neglected in the West where we have tended to associate the Last Supper with Good Friday more than Easter. It is not surprising that we have seen in the last few years what may be an equally one-sided emphasis on such words as "joy," "celebrate," and "rejoice." For so many centuries, western Christianity has associated the Lord's Supper primarily with words such as "repent," "broken," and "shed" that we take it for granted that it is a funeral meal. In some parts of Europe people wore their mourning clothes to communion. We need to balance the sorrowful aspects with the thankful and joyful praise that resounds in the eastern churches.

Another dimension is a strong sense of communion fellowship. "The bread which we break, is it not a participation [koinonia] in the body of Christ? Because there is one bread, we who are many are one body, for we all partake of the same bread." (I Corinthians 10:16b-17.) The Lord's Supper is the sacrament of unity in Christ for all those who, through baptism, have been incorporated into his church.

At the same time it is a commemoration of the past: "Do this in remembrance [anamnesis] of me." (I Corinthians 11:24.)

[19] We follow here the approach of Yngve Brilioth, *Eucharistic Faith and Practice, Evangelical and Catholic.*

Commemoration is the historical element, but it operates in a much wider sense than recalling the passion, death, and resurrection of Jesus. The Lord's Supper commemorates Christ's works from creation to the end of time, all of which are thankfully remembered in the Lord's Supper.

Theological controversies have abounded concerning the proper fashion of speaking of the Lord's Supper as a sacrifice. Probably most Christians would be willing to speak of the Lord's Supper as a memorial of Christ's sacrifice. Or most would agree in considering the sacrament a "sacrifice of praise" (Hebrews 13:15). It can also be seen as the Church's offering of herself in unity with Christ's eternal sacrifice on our behalf. The Lord's Supper is not a repetition of Calvary, but fear of such a doctrine should not blind us to the realization that the church has used sacrificial language with regard to this sacrament ever since the second century. The cost of our salvation is memorialized when we recall the sacrifice of Christ.

Equally important and equally theologically controversial is the sense of the presence of Christ. How are: "this is my body . . . , this is my blood" (Mark 14:22, 24) to be understood? We cannot neglect the presence of Christ simply because of unsatisfactory attempts to rationalize the Presence, whether in the Scholastic form of transubstantiation or in the Enlightenment direction of memorialism. It is hard to improve upon Calvin's confession that the manner in which we feed on Christ is "a secret too lofty for either my mind to comprehend or my words to declare . . . . I rather experience than understand it." [20]

There are, undoubtedly, other dimensions to the Lord's Supper. Some might add forgiveness of sins or eschatological expectation. But the five we have listed seem to summarize best the biblical witness. It is important in estimating the sign value of the Lord's Supper, as we practice it, that all five dimensions be kept in mind. History has shown that it is easy for one to crowd out the others and thus to distort the full meaning of the sacrament.

This is a very real problem in recent experimentations. It

[20] *Institutes,* IV, xvii, 32, McNeill and Battles edition, II: 1403.

is common for people to do a "communion service" using potato chips and coke instead of bread and wine. They use the rationale that these are modern equivalents and that a group closely united today would use such foods in a fellowship meal. This is fine as far as it goes, but it does not go far enough. Potato chips and coke highlight the element of fellowship, certainly an essential dimension of the Lord's Supper and one seriously neglected during the Middle Ages. But these substitutes almost completely obliterate the other dimensions. Who would connect potato chips and coke with Christ's real sacrifice, real to the point of giving up his body and blood, on our behalf? Who would associate feeding on Christ with potato chips and coke? And what Christ event do these snacks commemorate? They hardly recall the Last Supper. Even the element of thanksgiving is slighted since wine is much more festive. One thing is clear here, a coke is not "the real thing."

These sign-activities, the sacraments, must be used in their fullness rather than partially. This produces tensions, as some things have to give way a bit so as not to obscure others. To concentrate wholly on the fellowship aspect (however successfully) means actually losing more ground than gaining it. Once again we find that the sacraments go deeper than our ability to fathom them. We do best to give a well-rounded presentation of them as they have emerged in Scripture and tradition.

We can best examine the sign value of the Lord's Supper by beginning with the setting. Immediately we face some special problems since the Lord's Supper, as its name indicates, is a meal, and most meals have an intimate domestic quality. Yet here is a form of worship performed with hundreds, even thousands, of worshipers. It is a paradox, for the intimacy of the Passover meal (or other Jewish meals) was jealously guarded. The upper room was intended to be a definitely private dining room on the occasion of the last supper. It is not easy to translate this domestic privacy into a dining hall seating hundreds of people. We shall discuss the Lord's Supper as if we were preparing a banquet for the people of God.

At the center of any meal is a table. A table spread with a tablecloth immediately suggests eating. Though the last supper certainly did not look anything like Leonardo da Vinci's painting of it, the centrality of the table is obvious. (It is more likely that the diners at the last supper reclined—John 13:23 —around a "D"-shaped table, as depicted in early Christian paintings.) We begin, then, with a table that looks like a place where one may eat. It is not a little end table or buffet but a dining table where the family of God meets to feast.

Its form can vary, just as dining tables have taken various shapes at different times but each recognizable as a dining table in its age. At the same time, this is a place where prayer, praise, and thanksgiving are offered to God, and the act of offering may be signified by an altar form. The concept of the union of the church's sacrifice of praise with Christ's offering of himself on our behalf is worth maintaining. This may best be done with an altar-table form that suggests both an altar and a table. It can rest on a solid cube in the center with the slab projecting as at a table where people sit.

The altar-table is not placed in the church as a monument or as an architectural focus of the building. Its size does not depend on the size of the building but on its use. Five or six feet in length is plenty unless people are to sit about it. It should be scaled to a human being who presides at it rather than to the building that shelters it. The altar-table is a sign that is used, not one that is merely seen. When in use, it should be covered with cloth that looks like a good white tablecloth. There are better places to display textile art than by hiding the altar-table with a cloth frontal. Other than a tablecloth, little should be placed on the altar-table. Candles may be used as festive decorations. They were placed on the altar-table originally so the priest could see, and we now have more effective ways of lighting. But when we are festive (as at a banquet), candles may be placed on or around the altar-table. The number of them signifies nothing special except that each one adds one more candlepower. Books, offering plates, and flowers belong elsewhere, when possible. They clutter up and conceal the action.

Besides preparing the table, we must think about the people whom we have invited. Obviously the best pattern would be to have them around the table. The basic pattern for a church in which only the service of the table was celebrated would be a concentric one with the congregation all the way around the Lord's table except at the side where the presiding minister stands. A church designed this way would be much too limited to be feasible for other purposes, especially preaching. So we have to reach a compromise. Rather than moving the table into the center, we bring the people to it. Those communicating stand, sit, or kneel about it. Until the nineteenth century, Scottish Presbyterians set up tables in the aisles of the churches, placed benches around them, and all sat about these tables for the sacrament. The pew communion that replaced it (for reasons of convenience) was a much weaker sign of unity. (Sitting at tables is still practiced at communion in the Netherlands Reformed Church.)

Certainly the altar-table ought to stand free from the wall, so the minister may face across the altar-table his community gathered for the Lord's Supper. No one would turn his back on his guests, and it is distressing to see in many Protestant churches an altar built in medieval fashion against the wall of the church. Such altars are no longer permissible in new Roman Catholic churches. Anyone who has presided over the Lord's Supper, facing his people across the table, is hardly likely to relish an arrangement that makes such rapport impossible.

We must think in terms of people. The altar-table space is people's space, not monumental space. We have expressed too often a false sense of holiness, forgetting that it is the holy people who sanctify the place, not the altar-table. The dining-room is the cultic center of our homes because here the family congregates. Very likely it is the only place in the house where the family comes together regularly to do something in common. The family meal helps constitute the family as much as anything in modern society. Just so, the Lord's Supper helps build up the family of God. Space for the people about the altar-table is a strong sign of fellowship and unity in Christ. Such space should be ample, uncluttered, inviting, and easily accessible as if to bid welcome to all who come to the Lord's table.

Of course we think of food and drink whenever we entertain. Perhaps since the first century, the Lord's Supper has been a stylized meal with only bread and wine given. This was, perhaps, necessary and inevitable with the growth of the church. But at least we can make sure that these two elements are genuine food and drink. For the bread to have its highest sign value, it ought to be real bread recognizable as such by sight, touch, and taste. Unsliced bread is often available at local bakeries or can be made by church members. One of the important actions of the Lord's Supper depends on the availability of genuine bread. A major portion of the Christian churches has always used leavened bread, and there is no doubt about its orthodoxy. Unleavened wafers or cubes are poor substitutes for real bread.

About three quarters of the Protestant churches in this country have switched from the universal use of wine to grape juice within the past hundred years. We might presume that table wine became equally remote from the congregation's diet during this period. At least "the fruit of the vine," fermented or unfermented, ought always to be used at the Lord's Supper. It would seem foolish to reinstitute fermented wine where it would raise anxieties, since the sign value would be far from unitive. But it would also seem foolish to use grape juice when wine is acceptable to all.

Nor should we be ungenerous hosts, content with small portions. A single loaf of bread can be broken into fairly large portions unless more than two hundred communicants are present. The Puritans sometimes drank from beakers that allowed much more than a mere sip of wine. Even the containers help signify a meal. The best bread plates are not found in church goods stores but as decent baskets or trays sold as housewares. The wine may be kept in glass decanters or in original containers, if attractive, so it can be seen and heard as it gurgles out through the narrow neck. The sound of wine being poured is part of a festive occasion. The sign value of these vessels says eloquently: "Take and eat . . . , drink this."

Lastly one thinks of the room. Are there appropriate decorations for the occasion? Should we hang some banners, pictures, posters, or other visual arts calling our attention to the Lord's gift through this sacrament? Maybe we want candles and flowers scattered around where they will not get in the way but will add to the joy of the Lord's banquet. And then all things are ready. If we prepare this carefully for a social meal in our home and consider the sign values of hospitality so important there, how much more important are they in church at the Lord's Supper?

We have said before that the Lord's Supper is basically action and attempted to demonstrate this somewhat in Chapter V through the account of the "Silent Service." We turn now to discussing the sign value of the key actions. In our discussion of physical movement in the divine office we have already covered the actions of the service of the Word.

The Lord's Supper revolves around four sign-acts or, rather, clusters of activities: offering, giving thanks, breaking of bread, and giving. They, too, bear a parallel to our actions in serving a meal but have an even more powerful sign value as representations of the actions of Jesus at the last supper. These actions can be important sign-activities in communicating meaning or, through indifference or carelessness, can communicate little or nothing.[21]

The first of the actions is designated by the verb "to take" in the Gospel accounts. It is an action of preparation for the meal. We begin a meal by preparing the table and placing the food on it. In the Lord's Supper more happens, for it is a meal to which we all contribute. In the early church everyone brought bread and wine and they were collected to be used for the communion. The bread and wine come from us all and signify our offering.

This is best shown forth by having the bread and wine on a small table near the entrance to the church throughout the service of the Word. At the offertory, they are brought forward along with money and handed to the minister at the Lord's table. This is a more expressive action than having the bread and wine previously brought in from a sacristy and left on the altar-table. Sometimes a family may bake the bread and prepare the wine and can bring it forward, representing the congregation in this act of offering. Otherwise a cross section of the congregation—men, women, and children—ought to bear

[21] Cf. the detailed discussion of these actions in the Methodist rite by Joseph D. Quillian, Jr. in *Companion to the Book of Worship*, ed. by William F. Dunkle, Jr. and Joseph D. Quillian, Jr. (Nashville: Abingdon Press, 1970), pp. 60-71.

the elements. This is also a good time to have people stand and sing an appropriate offertory hymn.

Other actions occur at this time. The table may be spread— tablecloth and chalices—before the offertory procession reaches it. This will be considerably more complicated if individual glasses are considered necessary and that, apparently, depends on how devoutly members of the congregation believe in germs. (Episcopalians apparently are not dying off any faster than Methodists.) If individual glasses are not used, this may be the best time to pour the wine from its decanter or bottle into the chalice or chalices. Some would prefer to have the pouring out of the wine accompany the breaking of bread later. The table is set now and the Lord's feast is ready.

We next return thanks or, as we often say, "have the blessing." This is obviously a verbal part of any meal. To bless is to give thanks, and the great prayer of thanksgiving (or anaphora, canon, prayer of consecration, or great prayer) articulates the returning of thanks. It is expressed primarily in words, but actions can accompany it too. In many denominations, the rubrics include the manual acts which are a mime of Christ's actions. The minister, while reciting the narrative of the last supper, takes the bread and then the cup in imitation of Christ. Another possibility is the *orantes* position with the minister's arms outstretched and palms raised toward heaven slightly above shoulder height. Many Christians remain kneeling or seated and bowed during this prayer with their eyes either closed or glued to their prayer books. They would do better to stand and listen to the giving of thanks, as at the dinner table.

One of the oldest names for the Lord's Supper is the breaking of bread (Acts 2:42; 20:7). As the name suggests, it is a powerful way of signifying the sharing in the meal. Here is a utilitarian action that has also tremendous sign value. It is necessary to break the bread before we eat just as one has to carve the meat at dinner. But the breaking of the loaf of bread into two or more pieces also suggests the unity of the church in Christ. It often works well to repeat here Paul's words about the sharing in the one loaf (I Corinthians 10:16b-17). And some would pour the wine here, using I Corinthians 10:16a or a reference to Christ's pouring out of his blood for us. Others may argue that there is no need for words, that the action itself (when performed with a loaf of unsliced bread) is sufficiently eloquent.

Finally comes the time to eat and drink. The bread and wine are given. "To give" is an important verb that can be dramatized. We do not take the bread or wine, it is given to us. The minister, who unavoidably represents Christ to us as host of the meal, gives the bread and wine into our hands. St. Cyril of Jerusalem expressed the peoples' preparation for this action in fourth-century language: "Make thy left hand as if a throne for thy right, which is on the eve of receiving the King." [22] We receive; it is given. It is helpful to show people how to cup their hands to receive the bread, and to suggest ungloved hands. If a loaf of bread is used, a piece is broken off and the minister places it in the hands of people as he moves down the line of people kneeling at the rail or as a line of standing people approach him. The minister, as he gives the bread, would do well to touch each hand into which it is placed so that there is the warmth of person-to-person contact in giving. It is easy to determine the size to break the pieces by noting the number of those yet to commune. Often one uses up almost all the loaf. Words of administration may accompany the giving of the bread and wine, but they may say less than the acting out of Christ's giving himself for us and to us.

The giving of the cup is more difficult. Few would want a loaf passed hand to hand, and it is best for the minister alone to give the bread. But it is quite possible for people to minister the chalice or glasses to one another, especially if they stand about the altar-table. Some churches will prefer the individual glasses, though they have been an object of derision from the youth lately. In some congregations, a chalice with a pouring lip is used to pour into each cup, picked up empty from a tray near the entrance to the chancel. This preserves somewhat the sense of sharing from a common chalice. Many churches use intinction where each person dips his piece of bread into the wine. When this method is used, it is helpful for the minister to carry a napkin, holding it between the chalice and a person's

[22] St. Cyril of Jerusalem's Lectures on the Christian Sacraments, ed. by Frank L. Cross (London: S.P.C.K., 1960), p. 79.

lips, to prevent the wine from dripping. The unity is best signified in groups where each person feels free to drink from the same chalice. Obviously those who have a cold would intinct rather than drink from the chalice.

These are the four central actions of the Lord's Supper. Our gifts of bread and wine—one may almost say our lives—are taken, blessed, broken, and given back to us in Christ. It is a reenactment of what it means to be a Christian. Christ gives himself to us through these actions so that we can give ourselves to one another. We are made one with him that we may be one with one another and sense our oneness with all his creatures.

One negative sign ought to be avoided. We do not usually invite guests to watch us do the dishes. The disposal of the elements that remain need not take place during the service. But they ought to be disposed of in a reverent way after the service rather than gobbled up in a mad scramble of children or tossed into the garbage. After the service, members of the congregation can join the minister in consuming the remaining elements. Or they may be taken home and eaten at the family table. Another possibility is pouring the wine on the ground and scattering the bread crumbs on the earth.[23] The elements ought to be treated with as much respect as we would the Bible lest we undercut their power as signs. It is no wonder that small children sometimes think of communion as a snack for parents when they see how the remaining elements are treated.

It is important to realize that the sacraments are sign-activities which God has given to the church in order that we might better perceive his love. They are indeed "outward and visible" but we cannot act as if that made them any less "inward and spiritual." That would be untrue to human life, and we have to realize just how human the sacraments are. There is a unity in the sign-activity and the reality we perceive. And so it is most important that the sign-activity be allowed its full expression. After all, God became a man.

[23] Cf. Gordon Rupp, "Ablutions and the Methodists: Some Comments and an Outline for an Experimental Rite," *London Quarterly and Holborn Review* (October 1966), 276-80.

VIII
PREACHING

For the last half century, there have been continual lamentations over the decline of preaching. Preachers are prone to mourn the passing of the age of preaching giants whether they equate that age with Fosdick, Brooks, Finney, or Wesley. They scan the future of preaching with great concern. We hear that people do not respond to preaching the way they used to do. But we shall suggest that this is not necessarily a cause for gloom and may even be our greatest hope. Frankly, we are optimistic about the future of preaching, provided the sermon continues to be as adaptable as it has in the past.

It is no wonder that the preacher feels threatened today when he surveys the new forms of communications technology has provided. The "threat" of television has led to much wringing of hands. It certainly is a blow to pastoral visitation, but television may teach us how preaching can fulfill its highest potentialities in and for our age. The new communications mix may help us make preaching more relevant to our new cultural situation if we are willing to learn from our times and unlearn from the past. The sermon has probably had to change more often than any other part of worship. We still sing eighteenth-century hymns and recite sixteenth-century prayers, but such a time lag in preaching would be unthinkable. Change in preaching may well be a sign of its enduring vitality.

We can begin by inquiring as to what is distinctive about preaching. In briefest terms, we can define preaching as public speaking based on the trust that God gives himself to men through a specific communications medium: the spoken word. It involves nothing strange or esoteric, only the most common form of human communication—words spoken by ordinary human beings to other people. We might call preaching a risk that God takes. It is indeed risky business to entrust his word to men. But God apparently takes that risk. The Scriptures are full of instances of God putting his word into the mouths of men, many of whom recoil and rebel from the very thought of such responsibility. We can hardly say it better than Calvin: "For, among the many excellent gifts with which God has adorned the human race, it is a singular privilege that he deigns to consecrate to himself the mouths and tongues of men in order that his voice may resound in them." [1] Thus again, God "provides for our weakness" as he does with sacraments.

Preaching is a form of communication based on conviction that God is involved in the process as well as man. It is, we trust, a three-party form of speaking—God, preacher, and congregation. This definitely does not mean that such a connection is absent in other forms of speech, but that through preaching we are more apt to perceive the true quality of all words spoken in love, judgment, and reconciliation. We hold a high doctrine of the presence of Christ in preaching and look at preaching as a divinely given sign-act, a parallel to the sacraments.

Preaching is distinguished from ordinary speech in other ways. It usually occurs in public worship. The context is even more specific than that. That context is the relation of preaching to the public reading of Scripture. In the second century, Justin Martyr tells us, after "the memoirs of the apostles or the writings of the prophets are read, . . . the president in a discourse invites [us] to the imitation of these noble things." [2] The practice, of course, goes back much earlier to the synagogue (Luke 4:16-30). Two segments of the service of the Word or divine office are intimately related: the reading of the Scriptures and the contemporizing of them through preaching. The historic word and the contemporary one complement each other. Either one suffers when it stands alone in worship. It

---

[1] *Institutes IV*, 1, 5, McNeill and Battles edition, II: 1018.
[2] "First Apology" in *Early Christian Fathers*, p. 287.

is confusing to the congregation to allow other portions of the service—creed, hymns, prayers, offerings—to intrude between the two words, the lessons, and the sermon. Preaching in worship is shaped by its context as counterpart to the reading of Scripture lessons. We really should speak of the service of the Word in its entirety and not just of preaching as an isolated act. Nor do the two words complete the service of the Word. It also traditionally includes praise (before and between the lessons) and prayer (after the sermon). But we shall disregard this wider context for the immediate one, the juxtaposition of lessons and sermon.

We must ask why Scripture lessons have been the normal accompaniment of preaching in worship throughout the history of the church. The lessons are read as the corporate memories of the community of faith. Scripture consists primarily of those memories, once largely oral but now all written, which the Christian community cherishes as providing the key to history. In these events of the history of certain times and places, the church sees a disclosure that unlocks the meaning of all history. Past, present, and future history are illumined by the historical events narrated and reflected upon in Scripture. The church finds insight into all history through its understanding of God's purposes revealed in a definite and limited segment of history. The memory of these events and reflection on their meaning became Scripture.

The church is built up through the reiteration of these memories in its worship. Just as we rediscover what it is to be an American by commemorating the events of 1621, 1776, or 1918, so the church, too, rediscovers itself by rehearsal of its history, or at least crucial segments of it. The recalling of memories is unitive, it gives us a fresh look at what we have in common just as a family looks through its photograph album from time to time. The recital of our common memories unites us more firmly to one another through fresh sharing in our common heritage.

This is why nonscriptural lections cannot replace the biblical lessons; the two do not function the same way. Some experimenters introduce nonscriptural readings into worship in place of the biblical ones. This comes from failure to understand the role of the scriptural lessons reinforcing the church's corporate memories. Indeed, the substitutes often function in a contrary way because if they have any force—and who would want tame ones?—they are apt to be divisive. A reading from Martin Luther King, Robert Kennedy, or Dietrich Bonhoeffer is by no means apt to pull together all the worshipers in the average church. Such readings may provide excellent calls to confession or intercession, parts of the sermon, or offering of one's efforts. But they do not rehearse common memories and build up the church in the way that the canonical writings do. We are not arguing against noncanonical writings in worship but against substituting them for Scripture as lessons. A selection from the newspaper may effectively call us to confession; some days it can hardly do otherwise. A passage from Corita Kent may lead us to offer intercession with understanding. These materials do not function the way that biblical materials do in testifying to those special events the church has considered to be meaning-events that disclose God's purpose.

The lessons do not stand alone any more than the sermon does. The service immediately moves from the lessons to the exposition of their meaning for contemporary life. Sometimes the sermon is based explicitly on the lessons or a biblical text announced for the occasion. Sometimes the relation to Scripture is implied rather than explicit. At any rate, the sermon usually comes in the context of recital of how the church remembers God's actions in the past and moves to interpret his will today in the here and now. Though usually based on Scripture, the sermon moves to matters directed to human life in the present. The preacher must also read God's other book, the lives of our contemporaries.

Preaching combines the book of the Bible and the book of human experience, but in a most unbookish form. A sermon is not just words read from a manuscript. That is only the lifeless carcass of a sermon. A sermon is words spoken between persons. It is entirely different from something one can read at his own direction, at his own speed, in his own private way. Reading isolates us, preaching unites us. Reading makes us independent of others. Preaching is a social act.

The spoken word is communication through an entire person. When the lessons are read from the Bible, they become something more than they are when read in silence. The reading itself is interpretation through the voice and body of the reader. He may not be consciously or deliberately interpreting but inevitably he colors in the meaning of what he reads in the minds of the hearers. Many of us have been startled to hear things in a lesson when someone else reads it during a service that we did not hear, though we pondered the same words all week in preparing our sermon.

In the sermon, too, our whole being communicates. This is one reason it is so important that the hearer see the preacher and the preacher see his hearers. He is doing what a tape recorder cannot, giving his message through his total being as a person. "It is not too much to say that the minister as a man is a stronger witness to the Christian message than is the minister as a preacher." [3]

All that is a part of being man becomes a part of the act of preaching: one's past, present, and expectations. These are expressed by facial expressions, gestures, posture, as well as his voice. And the voice itself expresses far more than just words. Unfortunately many preachers never discover what a beautiful instrument the human voice is, far more expressive even than their hands. The human voice is capable of infinite varieties of speed, pitch, and volume. It becomes part of the sermon. One is less likely to be stirred by a well-written sermon if it is delivered in a high squeaky voice. And some badly written sermons have moved people largely by the power of the voice.

A whole human being is communicated in preaching. There are temptations here, grievous temptations to the preacher. It is at once the glory and despair of the preacher that he becomes identified with what he says and that what he says becomes identified with him. Only God would have entrusted so much to a mere man.

But it is not just a question of one man. A sermon is between people. There is no sermon if it is not heard. Words, yes, and gestures aplenty, but no sermon unless there are both preacher and hearer. A sermon is always a social event because it relates people to one another. Effective preaching is always based on this realization. The preacher develops a listener

[3] Ronald E. Sleeth, *Persuasive Preaching* (New York: Harper & Row, 1956), p. 22.

psychology. He is hearing with his congregation as well as speaking to them. This is one reason why a manuscript can be such a barrier between people and preacher if it interferes with the preacher's ability to listen. A sermon exists in time and cannot be recovered once it is spoken. One hears it now or never. One has to forget that he is a reader and return to an oral culture, hearing his sermon as others hear it. He cannot look at it as a space object not lost as sound waves dissipate. The sermon continues the same functions it had in preliterate societies, whether preached today among primitive peoples in remote parts of the world or in urban America.

One of the most important gifts in preaching is the sense of timing. Preachers can profit from listening to comedians such as Bob Hope who are masters at timing. They know when a thing is heard and grasped so their punch lines are not wasted. Comedians seem to do more hearing than speaking. The sermon, at best, is an exchange between persons with the preacher relating all the time to his hearers.

Preaching, then, is distinctive both because of its context and the use it makes of the spoken word. Some may worry about the context but the medium of the spoken word ought not disturb us. We have said much in this book about other media of communication than the spoken word. Our age has brought into prominence a mix of media that is new and unique. The other media can no longer be safely ignored by those who plan worship. But that does not mean that the power of the spoken word as a medium of communication is being downgraded though it no longer has its former monopoly.

Any doubts about the power of the spoken word ought to be resolved by recollecting some recent speeches. "It is unrealistic to think that preaching is no longer an effective means of communication if you heard and saw the 'I've Got a Dream' sermon delivered in front of the Lincoln Memorial in 1963 by Martin Luther King." [4] President John F. Kennedy probably owed his election to the spoken word brought into the homes of millions via television. The power of the spoken word to motivate men to thought and action seems undiminished despite the competition of other media.

[4] H. Grady Hardin, *Perkins School of Theology Journal*, XXII (Spring 1969): 88-89.

Television, the most conspicuous of the news media, makes full use of the spoken word. In advertisements, where there is less necessity for the spoken word, it still is the form of pitch used with most irritating frequency. The personal witness, evidently, sells better than other approaches or the market researchers would have long ago eliminated it. Television has not lost faith in the spoken word as an important means of communicating. It can be argued that our often-heralded move to a postliterate society is a move to a more oral society, such as were preliterate societies.

The spoken word has a quality of immediacy that makes it unique. A sermon is used once and thrown away. We preach to a particular group of people in a definite place at a specific time. A sermon is preached to people here and now and then, is never repeatable. For never again do just the same people assemble in the same place with the same concerns. Never again does that same sermon happen.

This immediacy gives the spoken word its special power of being relevant and timely. The printed page cannot be reset so fast, the artist cannot prepare visuals so rapidly, few musicians could improvise so constantly. But the spoken word can immediately catch what is going on between people and deal with it precisely and thoroughly. It has all the advantages of timeliness and relevancy, so widely sought in our world. And so the spoken word, as used in preaching, has power to communicate undiminished by the fast-moving pace of modern communications. Indeed, it can and ought to thrive upon this pace.

I

Why, if all these things are true, is anyone concerned about the future of preaching? We have stated the positive case first because the possibilities for preaching can be affirmative. But it would be foolish to pretend that preaching does not face some very real problems that can greatly diminish its effectiveness. Preaching has proven itself adaptable to meet fresh challenges in the past, but we must deal now with the problems of the present.

Though the spoken word bears up well in the communications mix, we may be threatened with a saturation of speech. It is not so much a problem of weakness of this medium but of overabundance. When our congregations hear highly skilled speakers all week on television, it is a challenge to the man who preaches on Sunday to match such eloquence and persuasion. His business, too, is persuasion, but he often feels like an amateur competing with professionals who have so much skill in telling their audience what to buy, what to believe, and what to do. It is a clash between two kinds of preaching, one commercial and the other Christian. The Christian preacher has the right medium, but he cannot devote his entire time and a large budget to preaching while the hucksters of things and ideas have an abundance of both time and money.

The newer communications media have brought to light an increasing shift in the minds of people from the type of thinking we have assumed good preaching presupposed—a clear, consistent, consecutive presentation. The carefully worked-out logical prediction of a thesis seems to be increasingly pushed aside by the suggestive, the whimsical, the parable, the joke. We ask the youth a question and they answer us with a question. We go to a movie and musical pieces break in with no reference to the action. We once envisioned the sermon as an arrow moving steadily toward a target. But a more apt image today may be a number of darts hurled in the same direction.

We preachers have learned to build our sermon outlines in clear and precise progression. Suddenly we find many people, especially younger people, are not impressed by this. Strangely, their way of talking sounds more like Jesus' habit in the Fourth Gospel of answering questions he is not asked. If we listen to the records the youth prefer, we do not get anything very consistent or clear, to say the least. We may get what they are saying by intuitions or "vibrations," but it is not the orderly way we were trained to preach. Somehow the youth get the message, almost by a magical osmosis so that suddenly they all think and feel the same thing from Tacoma to Tallahassee. Communication there undoubtedly is, but of a type that seems chaotic and disorderly to the middle-aged preacher. Perhaps our neat organization of ideas and careful avoidance of the nonsequitur is not quite so important as we once thought and worked so hard to make it be.

Another problem we need to consider is the relation of the present format of preaching to modern society. The basic difficulty here seems to be that preaching too often presents an image of authoritarianism rather than one of authority. Even the word "preach" often has this negative connotation in the modern world. "Don't preach to me" means "don't force your opinions on me." That is authoritarian, it is not persuasion on the basis of authority. Authority refers to respect for someone's command of his subject, an acknowledgment that "he knows what he's talking about." Jesus astounded people: "He taught them as one who had authority, and not as their scribes" (Matthew 7:29). Authoritarianism is a pose, resting on style and format rather than direct knowledge of the subject. It can and ought to be discarded without interfering with the authority of preaching.

We have a long history of an authoritarian format in preaching due to the previous relations of the church and culture. The church had its origins in the highly structured Roman world. In the early church, the bishop preached in each local congregation seated as the person who presided over the assembly. Literally he sat before (president) or chaired (chairman) the assembly. But when the church became respectable under Constantine and moved from private homes into sumptuous basilicas, the bishop simply assumed the throne the civil magistrate had occupied in such buildings.[5] The image of authoritarianism was beginning as church officials took on the badges of civil officials. But this made good sense in a rigidly structured society, both civil and ecclesiastical.

The pulpit evolved out of the ambo which had been designed for the reading of lessons, duplicating a similar desk and function in the synagogue. St. John Chrysostom in the fourth century supposedly began the utilization of the ambo for preaching as well as for reading. The late medieval pulpit became a majestic eminence (especially in the fifteenth century). It corresponded precisely to the role the priest played in

[5] James A. Whyte, "A Place for the Preaching of the Word," *Church-building*, 9 (April 1963): 5.

village life. The same reality, both physical and social, was preserved in the New England meetinghouse with the pulpit sometimes rising as high as fifteen feet from the floor. Here too, the minister remained a powerful factor in village life. The nineteenth century generally saw a lowering of these pulpits, partly because the choir and song leader now shared the platform and partly, no doubt, because the role of the preacher in an increasingly pluralistic society was less dominant. But stylistic revivals reversed that, and we got rid of the desk pulpit to return to gothic and Georgian pulpits, high and lifted up.

The problem, of course, is that these pulpits no longer reflect a social reality. They suggest a society with rigid social distinctions where the clergy had a definite prestige and power that has almost vanished in Protestantism and is disappearing rapidly in Roman Catholicism. They have become signs of authoritarianism in a society which is egalitarian. We are not condemning the pulpits of the past, for they reflected what was then a genuine social reality. But many pulpits of the present do not. J. A. T. Robinson lampoons our practice as preaching "six feet above contradiction." [6] Even the schoolmaster has come down off his platform so that teachers' desks are on the same level as the students. The high pulpit is a vestige of an authoritarianism that is no longer a social reality, as any preacher can testify.

The high pulpit also removes us from close contact with people. Some elevation is necessary in a long narrow church in order to be seen and heard from the back pews. But vertical separation is hard to overcome, especially for those in the front rows. Nor do massive pulpits relate us to people but instead suggest fortresses for protection. Like preaching robes, such pulpits may be a bit of cultural baggage from the past giving us an artificial security by clinging to the old format of authoritarianism. If these props exalted the Word, we would have no complaint but they seem more inclined to magnify the preacher.

One wishes that he could reach out and touch, both literally and symbolically, the people to whom he preaches. Most pul-

[6] The New Reformation? (Philadelphia: Westminster Press, 1965), p. 52.

pits are separated horizontally from the people to whom we speak by a moat of aisles and communion rails. The preacher often speaks twenty feet from the nearest human being. This physical remoteness enhances a false authoritarianism as if the preacher needed to keep his distance in order to retain our respect. All these project an image of preaching that is unrealistic for the modern world.

Contrast these relics of authoritarianism with genuine authority in preaching. When we were ordained, the bishop (presbyters or laity) very likely said something to the effect: "Take thou authority . . . to preach the Word of God, . . . in the congregation." This is authority not dependent upon social prestige or other cultural baggage but on being a true representative of the church and its faith. It comes after the ordinand has been examined as to his faith in the Scriptures and obedience to the doctrine and discipline of the church. He is not ordained to preach his own doctrine or that his parishioners might like to hear but the faith of the church as articulated in the Scriptures.

The authority of preaching consists in openness to the Scriptures and in openness to human beings. Genuine preaching has authority because it is a reflection of God's two books —Scripture and humanity. This is not a false authoritarianism, propped up by high pulpits, robes, distance, or other forms of security. The authority of preaching consists in its truthfulness to reality, in the preacher's ability to know first-hand what he is talking about.

Our times pose yet another problem for preaching. Preaching has been a "high definition" medium.[7] That is, preaching's content has been explicitly spelled out in detail so that the hearer brings comparatively little of himself to the medium. A glossy photograph is a high definition medium since it includes many details. A cartoon, on the other hand, is low definition since all that is provided is the outline and a few words. We have to fill in the details, the shading, and contrasts. We can do this because of certain conventions that we recognize to indicate movement, blushing, swearing, etc. A glossy photograph usually does not take much for granted.

[7] Marshall McLuhan, *Understanding Media*, p. 36.

We become more a part of a cartoon since we have to supply so much of it ourselves. Telephone conversation is another example of a low definition medium. Recently I had two occasions when I had to call long distance business numbers. I discovered, only by inquiring, that in one instance I was talking to a woman in Salt Lake City and in the other case, to one in Chicago. All that I knew, either time, was that I was talking to a woman. I had no image of her age, appearance, surroundings, or even her city (until I inquired). Contrast that with face-to-face conversation in which we see another person, his facial expressions, gestures, and surroundings. Much more is defined for us in this form of communication and less demanded of our imagination. At present, we seem to be moving to more reliance on low definition forms of communications, especially in television.

Preaching traditionally has been a high definition medium. We are told what to believe, feel, and do. Not only does the preacher exegete the biblical text, but he then proceeds to explain and apply it to our life situation. We take it all from him. There is little demand for us to become part of the preaching act. It is all done for us. We can take it or leave it. But we contribute remarkably little to the average sermon. It is all done for us and all we have to do is to stay awake. The preacher resolves the problems, connects the ideas, and fills in the gaps. He offers a package deal which we can accept or reject.

One of the major problems in preaching today is how to make it more of a low definition medium in which the congregation can feel the demand for its imagination and thinking to fill out the message. They must become more a part of the preaching act. Men are less content today to be uncritical receptacles for others' ideas. They want to be a part of the wrestling themselves. They are too old to be spoon-fed and want to do some real chewing. At least they want to make their applications to their own individual lives instead of having all this spelled out by another. Modern man often relishes the low definition approach because it takes more seriously his capacity to supply ideas and meaning from his own experience.

Closely akin to this is the problem that preaching, as we have known it, has taken the form of a monologue whereas normal speech is a give-and-take procedure. At best, recent preaching has been a silent dialogue. But when someone talks to us in conversation we talk back audibly. It is a two-way exchange verbally as well as by expressions and gestures. This has been lost in preaching. One person does all the verbalizing. No one talks back. The rest of us may respond by our expressions, postures, and even by an occasional snore. But as far as spoken words are concerned, preaching is a one-way communication, from the preacher to us but not vice versa.

Our grandfathers knew a better method. If they agreed with what the preacher said, they shouted "amen," and it has been a long time since we got a "hallelujah." Liturgically these expressions were excellent responses. But our sophistication and good taste have ruled out even these limited exchanges. One lacked a way of expressing his disagreement with the preacher (except for the offering) but at least had a way of verbally affirming what had been said. We might not care to go back to the "amen" during the sermon, though it would be encouraging to have the audible support of the congregation. The "amen" helped make the sermon, in an elementary way, a two-way form of speech.

Our problem remains how to get the sermon out of the pulpit and into the pew. It is not preached, after all, for the preacher's benefit alone but for the people, and they need to become more and more a part of the sermon. The sermon is something the preacher could share more with the congregation and they with him, did not our present forms of preaching inhibit this.

In short, the word must be heard, not just preached. The sermon must be heard by the people in the pews so that it becomes a two-way form of communication. They must have voices too and not be simply subject to the pastor's monologue. We know how easy it is to tune out one person's speech. You can hardly do that in conversation; it is all too easy in a sermon.

II

These are genuine problems, to be sure, but new forms of preaching have developed in recent years as response to such challenges. We shall survey some of these practices. It should not surprise us that different styles of preaching are evolving.

This is nothing new. If we look at the great Puritan sermons of the seventeenth century, we wonder how people ever sat through such long discourses with their tedious division of texts. Of course we see only the printed words and not the flesh-and-blood reality of these sermons. But even that much looks far different from printed sermons of today. The camp-meeting sermon of the frontier has been replaced by the more sedate sermon of a settled community, reflecting a change in social realities. The preaching of the Franciscans was an innovation in the thirteenth century just as was that of the Wesleyans in the eighteenth. It is not surprising, then, that new forms of preaching are emerging when people are changing.

Preaching has always had to take seriously the situation and people present in worship. But we are apt to find a much greater variety of worship environments and more distinct types of people than we have experienced in the past. All we say about new practices assumes real sensitivity to the people present and the location of the service. The situation of preaching to a group of young adults in a dormitory room will certainly dictate the possibilities open—and closed—to us.

There are large numbers of people who see no need for change in preaching. The form of the sermons they hear seems natural to them. In some of the churches of the underprivileged, preaching has plenty of elements of spontaneity and excitement. For others, who relish a carefully planned and highly defined monologue, the sermon preached in the average suburban church is quite satisfactory. But these people are far from the whole population, even though they may be a majority of the people in the pews. Those who are satisfied may sense no need for change, oblivious to the fact that the sermons they hear have undergone slow but continual change during the last fifty years. They resent it when drastic change is suggested and are perfectly right in doing so, because the average sermon reflects the way they live and perceive things. Others may just be too gentle to tell us they are bored stiff with preaching as usual.

But there are many others, rarely troubled by subtlety these days, who are restless with preaching. These people, who may be the majority of the population, demand changes in the style of preaching if we are to reach them at all. The changes desired seem to be in the direction of more participation and involvement on the part of the congregation. Rather than a passive audience, soaking up the preacher's message, there seems to be developing a tendency toward preaching that is unauthoritarian in format, low definition in style, and dialogic in character. These features seem to run through most of the new experiments in preaching.

Some experiments have developed from recognition of our general failure to relate the process of Christian education and preaching. There ought to be an obvious reciprocal influence between preaching and the teaching of Christian doctrine.[8] Preaching and education ought to imply each other. Unfortunately there is little obvious connection between what goes on in the church classroom and what happens in the pulpit. It is a prerequisite of some of the new forms of preaching that this gap be bridged. In those traditions where a lectionary is used in worship, resolution of this problem may be easier. There, classroom discussions can revolve around points in doctrine, ethics, or church life raised by the texts for the day. Then the class has already begun to wrestle with these concerns before it hears the sermon. At one church college, the religion courses are structured around the liturgical epistles and gospels for the week.

In other traditions it may be possible for the minister and educational director to work out a combination of sermon texts or topics with the material studied by various age groups. Frequently, the sermon may have to adjust to current events but so can much of the teaching and classroom discussion. If a minister knew that the adult classes were studying the biblical texts on which he plans to preach, he might spend more time on careful exegesis. People will participate much more readily in a sermon that deals with texts or concerns to which they have already given thought.

It is helpful to begin looking at actual experiments by analyzing the physical setting of preaching. We have seen in the case of the sacraments how much this affects the meaning people will apply to an act of worship. The font and altar-table be-

[8] Cf. Heinrich Ott, Theology and Preaching (Philadelphia: Westminster Press, 1965), p. 24.

come important parts of the sacraments as sign-activities. This is no less true about preaching. One's image of preaching is very much tied up with the appearance and location of the pulpit. We may speak in symbolic terms, of trying to preach to people on their level, but this is easier to realize if we also literally stand on their level. It is amazing what a different act preaching becomes when the preacher physically comes down and stands on the same level as the congregation, or only as much higher as is absolutely necessary to be heard and seen in the rear of the room. Obviously this is much easier in a room where the back pews are not remote. Some of these experiments we shall describe demand that the minister leave his high pulpit and preach on the congregation's level.

A pulpit, whether movable or not, presents the possibility of making visible the relation between Scripture and sermon. Both altar-table frontals and pulpit hangings could give way to something with more important sign value. The most visible thing about the pulpit should be the Bible which is read there. One's image of preaching will be affected if he always sees the Bible while watching the preacher speak. If the Bible is placed on the side of the pulpit facing the congregation, the acts of picking it up to read, placing it on the desk of the pulpit, opening and closing it, and returning it to the congregation side underscore the nature of the lessons as readings of God's Word. A handsomely bound Bible is a delight to the eye and a more functional art form than a cloth hanging. The visual connection between Bible and preaching can help communicate the grounds for the authority of preaching to both preacher and congregation.

In looking at various experiments in preaching, we shall move in the direction of more and more "full, conscious, and active participation." The first, a relatively tame and conventional approach, involves the use of various techniques to get the congregation to raise questions for sermons. Obviously much present-day preaching grows out of individual requests of this type or needs that the pastor perceives in the course of his relations with his people. But there is much to be said for a more formal procedure that shows people one's concern that preaching be for them. Various ways can be conceived to enable people to put into writing the questions and concerns that they would like to see dealt with in sermons. Three-by-five cards could be dropped in the offering plate, mailed in, or handed to the pastor with requests for sermons. People will listen to hear not just what you have to say when you preach on their special concern but to hear also what their neighbors want to explore.

A further step is to ask people to put into writing their résumé and comments on the sermon after it has been preached. This is a touchy matter because one is not asking for criticism or praise but for reactions. Many people will greet the preacher at the door with a cheerful: "I enjoyed your sermon," though he may have preached on the damnation of the wicked. To put the response into anonymous writing may produce truer expressions. That is not really the point, though. The purpose of asking for a written comment is to stimulate the attention one gets when the hearer knows he will have to respond in some way. We definitely do not want people to take notes during the sermon. That is to substitute a different medium for the social encounter of preaching. But we do want the attention that can recall after twenty minutes something of what has been said. To give the congregation the responsibility of summing up the sermon in a few minutes' time immediately afterward is to raise the probability of heightened attention.

This same intention can be pushed further by having a discussion period on the sermon after the service is over. We want neither praise nor criticism but evaluation and application of the ideas. This may provoke more pointed and blunt sermons, but we have never had an overabundance of them. If substantial doctrinal and ethical issues are raised in the sermon, the discussion session can be vigorous. A good sermon does not end with the final "amen." A discussion session gives the possibility of talk-back and draws on the experience of a variety of individuals. It may be necessary to have several groups assemble in different places if the number who want to discuss is large. This practice has had considerable appeal among students who are rather adept at talking back.

Moving in another direction, we can find groups in congregations working during the week to discuss the text or even to prepare the sermon.[9] The minister functions as a coordinator and delivers the final product. Such a practice demands a group that is willing to take the time and effort to wrestle seriously with a text or problem. It takes a lot more time to prepare than the average sermon. But the process of biblical and theological study combined with discussion may be well worth the time it involves. It gives both people and minister a magnificent learning opportunity. Special skills are required to preach what is, in effect, a corporate sermon. The skills demanded include a bit of self-restraint in not creating something of one's own but of coordinating and expressing the work of others. At times the minister may be excited about the insights and experiences members of the group bring, but he may be perturbed at times over ideas about which he has doubts or reservations. We are so accustomed to the sermon being a solo act that it is indeed difficult to let go and to allow others to help prepare it.

In recent years, there have been numerous experiments with the dialogue sermon. Actually these are of many types.[10] They may include two ministers who use a question-and-answer technique or simply a rather conversational approach that the congregation, as it were, overhears. Sometimes the cast includes a layman who may stand up in his pew to raise questions of the preacher or even dramatically (the first time, at least) interrupt a sermon. Several people may raise questions or engage in discussion with the minister.

The chief value of the dialogue sermon is not its novelty or occasional excitement but the opportunity for people to identify with a position taken by one of the speakers. They, in effect, have gained a spokesman and are anxious to hear a certain view defended as well as challenged. "Yeah, that goes for me too," is a normal feeling during a dialogue sermon. Very often the two (or more) speakers will oppose a skeptical position to a believing one, or a literalist approach against a critical

[9] George W. Webber, *The Congregation in Mission* (Nashville: Abingdon Press, 1964), pp. 82-84.

[10] Eight of these are illustrated by William D. Thompson and Gordon C. Bennett, *Dialogue Preaching: The Shared Sermon* (Valley Forge: Judson Press, 1969).

one (this is one way of making Jonah more than a fish story), or a liberal versus a conservative position.

No one should be made a straw man and ridiculed. If the positions are not genuine ones that can be held with integrity, it will soon be obvious. No one wins in a good dialogue sermon. There is usually truth in both points of view, and if that becomes evident it has been a success. If one position gets lampooned, members of the congregation who sincerely hold it may be insulted. A sermon on infant baptism may reflect two differing views as to its propriety, views widely held today in almost any denomination. Neither side is apt to prevail, but in the process of a dialogue sermon some real teaching about the meaning of baptism may result.

Dialogue preaching requires certain skills that not all of us have. It requires a certain amount of dramatic ability. Such sermons will suffer if one appears to be reading, though notes may be used. Spontaneity and the willingness to intrude with "now, just a minute, let me ask . . ." are almost requisite. On the other hand, too much aggressiveness or the attempt to dominate the situation must be resisted. And considerable imagination is needed to discover texts and topics on which there can be creative and sincere disagreement. We were not all made for this type of preaching, but it may be worth trying a time or two to find out. Knowing what not to do is sometimes half the battle.

A fuller form of involvement and participation occurs in the open-ended sermon. This moves even further in the direction of a low definition medium. It has a certain resemblance to Frank R. Stockton's story, "The Lady or the Tiger." In the open-ended sermon, the minister begins by interpreting a text or some commonly held belief, raises some problem with regard to it, maybe offers his own resolution of this, and then turns the sermon over to the congregation. Individuals stand up and contribute their witness to the interpretation of the text or belief in terms of their own lives and experiences.

This is a natural type of sermon to employ in small groups, but it may work well with as many as several hundred people if they are not too inhibited. It does require a minister who is fairly secure and willing to take the risk that almost anything might happen or nothing at all. And occasionally nothing will happen. No one will speak and there is nothing so frightening to ministers as nothing. But at other times the interest may be so high that it will be difficult to end the sermon on time so people can go home. The open-ended sermon means introducing a high element of chance and risk such as we are not used to in our worship. Even the dialogue sermon is firmly under the minister's control and can be tailored to last twenty minutes, no more and no less. We may question why worship always has to end at twelve sharp, no matter how dull. We never know when or where an open-ended sermon will end.

This type of sermon needs a text or common basis as a constant point of reference. The minister can use tools the congregation does not have in interpreting the text—Greek, Hebrew, and commentaries. He will probably have to articulate some of the salient problems in the text, but whether he gives his own resolution or not will depend upon the text.

The congregational witness is not meant to be praise or criticism of what the preacher has said but to draw on the experiences of individuals in the congregation. We ask for a wider witness than the reflections of any one individual, including the preacher, can provide. Even if the preacher were the most widely read, educated, or traveled person in the congregation, the experiences of others can supplement his.

Considerable skill is demanded in presiding over this type of expanded witness. The preacher's job is not to answer or reply to each statement but simply to say "thank you." Once he has introduced the sermon, he must be willing to let go of it. Of course, if there are questions he may answer them. He is presiding, not defending his interpretation. He must not dominate the action but be willing to let the people carry the ball. Sometimes he may have to exercise considerable diplomacy when there are conflicting witnesses, and he may have to flag down someone who is long-winded. People with prepared responses should not be planted in the congregation. This soon becomes obvious, though sometimes it is tempting to do so to lessen the risks.

The open-ended sermon ought not be used every Sunday, but it can have great value in making people sense themselves to be part of the sermon. It will be found that the imagination and preparation required often far exceed the work that goes into a conventional sermon. This type of sermon is no shortcut to hard work. Even when the result produces embarrassing silence, there may be considerable reflection stimulated. Even those who do not speak become real participants. And those who do speak may surprise us with their insights. A housewife may express concerns that unite the housewives but to which the minister and men in the congregation may be oblivious. Each such sermon is a unique happening, never repeated.

We can briefly give an example of a sermon of this type. It had two texts: John 2:15 and Matthew 5:39. One is an account of Jesus cleansing the temple, the other is the saying about turning the other cheek. Both texts were exegeted including explanation that the Johannine account is rather violent. (The same word—phragellion, phragellosas—is used in Greek for the whip with which Jesus drove out the sellers of animals, and in the account in Mark 15:15 of the soldiers whipping him.) The question was asked how these passages could be reconciled, and the resolution was offered that violence may be necessary for the good of others but not for ourselves. The sermon was then turned over to the congregation and various people began to stand. These were recognized and spoke in turn until it was necessary to call attention to the limitations of time. There were other occasions when little or nothing happened.

We must say a few words about the use of technical means, such as slides, movies, tapes, and various combinations of these, in sermons. Frankly, this is dangerous business. The power of these media is so engrossing that they can easily make the sermon seem pale by comparison. There may be occasions on which a single slide or a few slides may accompany a sermon. But motion pictures will not accompany a sermon; it instead will accompany the motion picture. There may be rare occasions in which a portion of a motion picture such as "The Gospel According to Saint Matthew" might replace the sermon. Motion pictures ought to be left for Sunday evening discussion groups or other occasions. At present we do not consider motion pictures an asset to preaching. Even when a few slides are chosen to support the sermon, they ought not draw attention to themselves but be subordinate to what is said. If we show a single slide of a war casualty, the emotional shock may be so great that nothing we say may be heard.

It seems likely that preaching will continue to adopt new forms in the future just as it has in the past. These experiments all suggest sermons that are less formal in structure and strive for relevance to the lives of the hearers. They seem to be more democratic, more low definition in approach, and involve two-way communication. Above all, they attempt to achieve a high degree of participation on the part of the congregation. Frequently they succeed in getting the sermon out of the pulpit and into the pew.

IX

THE WORDS OF WORSHIP

Most people who talk about new forms of worship think immediately of changes in the words used in worship. They often equate experimentation with the modernizing of the vocabulary of a worship service. If nothing else, this common identification of contemporary worship with updating the language shows us just how verbal our fixation has been.

To be sure, the words of worship are important. No one has any right to scoff at efforts aimed at securing a contemporary liturgical language. But we have argued in this book that there are other languages than verbal ones. These we have neglected in the past but are being forced to reconsider. The chief changes in worship in the immediate future appear to move in a nonverbal direction. To equate liturgical reform with publishing new liturgical texts now seems almost ridiculously naïve. We have neglected the languages of the environment, the body, the arts, and the sacraments so long that our biggest effort must be directed in those directions. We cannot limit ourselves any longer only to what can be compressed into words. To be sure, it would be much simpler if all we had to do was make certain that the verbal portions of worship reflected current realities. We must continue to work toward this too, but that alone no longer will be sufficient to enable contemporary man to express himself adequately in worship.

Accordingly, we have left until last our discussion of the words of worship. We do not intend to downgrade this subject but simply to reverse the usual priorities. Words are and will continue to be a primary vehicle for expressing our worship.

But the facile identification of worship with words is being questioned in our time.

Words are likely to continue to be the most versatile and precise forms of expression we have. Although the Quakers have been showing us for over three hundred years that we can worship in silence, few of us would care to eliminate words from our worship. The spoken and read word takes its place, no longer in isolation, but still at the head of the list of media that man can use to offer his worship to God.

The problems of religious language are much deeper than the problems of just liturgical language. Our scope will have to be much narrower than to attempt even the most rapid of surveys about hermeneutics or the varieties of "God-talk" available. These are matters of tremendous importance on which a vast literature has appeared which hardly needs duplication here. Instead we shall define the practical problems we face in the use of words in worship today. We shall suggest tentative solutions to some of these problems.[1]

Some of the problems are obvious, particularly those involved in the retention of sixteenth-century liturgical language. The case of The United Methodist Church is the most striking. Being one of the first churches to bring out revised worship texts in the 1960s, The United Methodist Church approved a new *Book of Worship* in 1964, only to discover within less than five years that other large denominations were on the verge of abandoning Edwardian language, largely due to the precedent of the Roman Catholic Church. The language of the 1964 *Book of Worship* retains many words and phrases that have survived alteration in the centuries since Thomas Cranmer and his associates published the first *Book of Common Prayer* in 1549, a date much closer in time to Chaucer (died 1400) than to us. Yet except for a few omissions (for theological reasons), only two words had been changed in the general confession, and only four in the Lord's Prayer, in 415 years.

The denominational and ecumenical revisions of liturgical books since 1964 have avoided retention of such language.

[1] For an interesting approach to these problems from an Anglican perspective, see Daniel B. Stevick, *Language in Worship: Reflections on a Crisis* (New York: Seabury Press, 1970).

Though the revisers have not agreed as to what constitutes contemporary liturgical prose, at least they concur that it no longer is Cranmer touched up. Strangely enough, this changed perspective is probably less apparent in those churches where prayer is prepared for each occasion by the minister. It is likely that he continues to pray in the language of his ancestors. As far as the words are concerned, prayer extempore is often not from the times in which we live.

The problems of language revision are manifold, and we can do little more here than to catalog them.[2] We begin with individual words that have changed their meaning since the Reformation. Many, though by no means all, of these words have been replaced in liturgical revisions in the past. Most striking are those words that have changed their meaning by a hundred and eighty degrees. "Let" once meant prevent. "Prevent" has changed its significance almost as much. Few people connect it with going before, a concept we now express with the word "precede." Fortunately most churches soon will cease to be "sore let and hindered" by these words. The phrase "the comfortable words" indicates to modern ears consolation rather than strengthening. We no longer "magnify the Lord" or seek the "inspiration of thy Holy Spirit." Many of these words evince the latinisms common in English at the time. Change has also occurred in the meaning of Old English words such as "whole." When our ancestors prayed for the "whole state of Christ's church" they were thinking of the health of the church. Only in church does "quick" still mean living. All these words remain perfectly good modern words, but they mean something quite different today.

The problem is simpler with another group of words, those no longer in contemporary use. We have somehow managed to adjust to using "beseech" or "vouchsafe" when we worship but would startle people if we used such words anywhere else but in church. Quaintest of all is the promise made at weddings when a couple promises to "give thee my troth." Such words

---

[2] Cf. the excellent study of many of these problems by Stella Brook, *The Language of the Book of Common Prayer* (London: Andre Deutsch, 1965). Though she deals with the *Book of Common Prayer*, most of the English-speaking churches derive their liturgical language from Cranmer and, consequently, this book deals with their history too.

and phrases retain more beauty than meaning. The problem of pronouns is familiar. We have become so accustomed to addressing God as "thee" or "thou" that we forget that this is a purely grammatical matter since these forms were common singular pronouns once used for addressing any individual. Since 1549 we have always used "you" forms for the plural: "Lift up your hearts." For better or for worse, the English language went the other way and "you" now covers both singular and plural. It takes almost a year of practice before most people feel natural addressing God as "you." Is it worth the effort? It is doubtful that any clarity would be gained by substituting "you" for "thou," but there is an advantage in making prayer sound more like ordinary speech and closer to daily life.

Verb forms create far more complications. The "-(e) st" second person singular ending ("didst," "hast") or the "-(e) th" endings of the third singular form of verbs ("hath," "passeth") sound quaint in worship and absurd elsewhere today. Generally prayer book English (by which most of us still pray whether from a book or not) was a bit conservative and avoided the modernism of the "-(e)s" endings for third person singular ("has" "passes"). They were a feature of northern dialects that still sounded a bit too colloquial for the refined ear. Strong verbs cause further complications: "God spake" or "he brake it." Trying to use unfamiliar forms in extempore prayer can sometimes lead to spectacular verbal gymnastics, especially when one tries to put a sixteenth-century ending on a verb that has not been inflected lately ("you spoke —thou spakest"). There seems to be no reason to retain these purely grammatical features of the sixteenth century.

More important than the changes in words has been the shift in language structure. This is often missed by those who think that the problem of liturgical revision consists simply in substituting new words for old. The way words are put together has altered drastically since the sixteenth century and must be recognized for what it is at heart, a change in ways of thinking about life.

Cranmer had few models for liturgical language in English. Most of his sources were in Latin, but the Latin prose was distinguished by "its capacity for compression, English in its capacity for amplification." [3] This English characteristic shows frequently in the doubling of words, linking new words of latinate and native origins. Not only words but whole clauses are balanced, as in the general confession from morning prayer, hardly changed since 1552:

> *Almighty and most merciful* Father, we have *erred and strayed* from thy ways like lost sheep. We have followed too much the *devices and desires* of our own hearts . . . . *We have left undone things which we ought to have done, and we have done those things which we ought not to have done.*

That is undoubtedly beautiful, but it is definitely not the way men speak or write today. If we can say something in one word instead of three, we say it that way. We are impatient with superfluous verbiage and prefer utility to elegance. The parallelisms of the sixteenth century sound stuffy and pompous to modern man.

More subtle but equally characteristic of Cranmer's language are the patterns of stress on syllables so that passages read with a cadence of charm and beauty. As revisers have found, when they begin to change a word or a phrase the whole thing falls apart. Sixteenth-century writers had a tremendous asset in the closeness of written English to that spoken.

Writers of this period were not so far removed as we are from the normal medieval practice of reading aloud (even in private) and hence of writing for the ear. We take for granted a divorce between written and spoken styles that is especially baffling for those who write liturgical texts. These must combine both written and spoken styles, yet it often seems like trying to stand in two boats as they drift apart. The eye demands sustained and grammatical logic, the ear liveliness and variety of expression. (If anyone doubts that these two styles have been put asunder in the twentieth century, he should try turning lectures into a book.) It may be that the emergence of good liturgical prose in our time will have to await the reuniting of written and spoken English.

[3] *Ibid.*, p. 128.

Characteristic of prayer book prose is the use of relative clauses, particularly in the collects. These make very good sense in Latin and reflect the continuity of a tradition going back at least to the fifth century. God is addressed, then spoken of in a relative clause. To us it seems strangely awkward. We would hardly say, "Miss Smith, who teaches fourth grade, we would like to talk with you in order that we can better understand our boy, Johnny." All these words are contemporary, the structure is archaic. It might delight the sixteenth-century ear, it troubles us.

These changes in the way words are put together reflect changes in our thinking. Behind these carefully wrought phrases is an assumption of order and coherence in a society firmly structured. Balance and symmetry make sense in a harmonious universe with a place for everything and everything in its place. Everything is done "decently and in order" in the world as well as in the liturgy.

This is even more apparent in the hymnody of the eighteenth century when men found it natural to express their thoughts in neat classical patterns of recurring meter. These hymns could be easily set to music because the stanzas repeated familiar patterns of common meter, short meter, long meter, or whatever. The cosmic confidence many of these hymns radiate seems alien to us. We can only stammer out our perplexities in loosely organized free verse. As a result, we cannot write new hymn texts the way eighteenth-century man did without sounding glib and superficial. We begin thinking today with different assumptions about life than our ancestors had in the sixteenth or eighteen centuries. And so we put words together in different ways.

A further area of difficulty is with regard to the imagery we use in our languages. Until the eighteenth century, most people in England and America were country dwellers. The phrases that came naturally to their minds were rural in content. In this they had not changed much from the days of the Bible, and so biblical images had a real immediacy to them. One summer I lived on a sheep ranch and came to realize how the Bible abounds in images of shepherdy and how apt they are. When one has taken a lamb to the slaughter, he realizes what a powerful image "led like a sheep to slaughter" is. Many of these biblical images are foreign to the experiences of modern urban man. City children might be more frightened than a ewe if suddenly confronted by one.

On the other hand, it is easy to magnify the meaninglessness of many of these images. Part of the biblical power to communicate lies in the universality of experiences: a lost coin, a run-away son, war and suffering, childbirth and death. And television has magnified our range of experience. Adults may wonder whether a child can grasp a reference to a potter at his wheel, only to discover that the child has seen one on television and understands it better than his parents. They may even know more about sheep. The religious images in the Bible seem most puzzling, those of redemption (trading stamps), sacrifice (bargain), and priest (the occult). But fortunately the Bible is not a very religious book; its images are from everyday life and we may do too much complaining about their incomprehensibleness.

At any rate, we are stuck with the biblical images and we could do far worse. New translations do a great deal to make sense of these images. *The Jerusalem Bible* or *The New English Bible* sometimes make images we once considered worn out sound strikingly contemporary.

The imagery of our hymns is often less possible to recover. Most of the hymns we sing come from the eighteenth and nineteenth centuries. They sometimes seem more archaic than the much older biblical images. In days when carcasses were dipped in the market fountain, one could sing of "a fountain filled with blood/Drawn from Emmanuel's veins." It is doubtful one can today. Some hymns such as "O God, Our Help in Ages Past" and "O for a Thousand Tongues to Sing" more than compensate for a few obsolete images ("the watch that ends the night" "charms our fears.") We can continue to sing these with sense.

Fortunately, in the case of hymns, there is no reason why we should be stuck with those that no longer have meaning. Our hymnals have embalmed many when a good burial would have been better. There is no need to keep alive hymns whose imagery is moribund. Rather than practice vain repetition, we can discard those hymns that only communicate the irrelevancy of our faith.

There is also the problem of a whole world view that has changed. This has been discussed at length by biblical scholars and theologians. Its impact on worship is probably obvious. We approach God largely through the etiquette of court ritual. Our whole form of speech presumes a world of kings and empires though these no longer correspond to things we know directly. Ancient forms of reverential address in prayers become increasingly opaque, and change is long overdue if only we knew what to substitute.

Some of the changes of world view are less obvious but equally important. If one looks through collections of gospel hymns, he finds about one half of the hymns begin with the word "I." They reflect a type of society that idealized the rugged individual who could be self-reliant and ignore his neighbors. In many of these hymns, the church seems to be little more than an option for the Christian. Today the Christian life seems to center in the church community. Missionary hymns of the last century reflect a patronizing of other races that now makes us squirm. The whole world view these words express has changed, and so the words are no longer tolerable in Christian worship.

There are many problems with the language of worship that we have inherited. Changes in word meanings, language structures, imagery, and world views have been so widespread that much of the old liturgical language is no longer adequate for expressing our insight into God and response to his activity. It is easy to recognize these shortcomings in the words of worship; it is far more difficult to know which way to turn in order to overcome them.

I

We would be happy if we could stop at this point and resolve the problems of the language of worship by attention to overcoming stylistic difficulties. Unfortunately the problems of form only lead us to deeper problems of content. What we say is so deeply associated with how we say it that the two can hardly be separated. Form and content of language go hand in hand.

In some parts of worship, the problem of content is much

less a difficulty than in others. We have givens in some areas where the content is already determined. The Scripture lessons are examples where our problem is not to produce new substance but to find the most adequate translation available. This involves us in comparison of the possibilities now open but is hardly a case of having to create something new. The same is true of the creeds. New translations made by Catholic and Protestant scholars working jointly are available.[4]

We have noted the flood of new hymns now appearing. One can easily get tired of being told that all we need is love, and some of the texts and music are as banal as much popular music. Obviously discernment is needed in selecting those hymns with serious texts set to appropriate music. There are solutions, not always happy solutions, but at least some are available in the areas we have mentioned.

The real problem area is the language of prayer. The crisis in liturgical language has revealed something that we covered up as long as we were content with sixteenth-century language. "We do not even know how we ought to pray." It is by no means a new problem but has always been with the church. But we have managed to conceal it from ourselves for quite a time. Changing sixteenth-century words for twentieth-century ones has revealed to us our poverty in this area. Once we start exchanging old words for new ones, we realize that there were confident realities beneath sixteenth-century cadences that have since evaporated. New styles make poor wineskins for old contents. Not until we realize that the crisis in the language of prayer is one of content and not merely of form, can we attempt to deal with the words of prayer.

Part of the difficulty is that we think of prayer as exclusively verbal. Most Protestants admire, but cannot share, the Quaker's silent waiting on God. Periods of silence in Protestant worship often degenerate into daydreaming unless a bidding prayer or some such form is imposed. We have not regained any sense of praying with our body. The rosary has died in Catholicism at about the time the youth have picked up oriental disciplines in which the body creates part of the rhythm of

[4] *Prayers We Have in Common* (Philadelphia: Fortress Press, 1970), pp. 9-14.

meditation. But for us the problem of prayer remains that of finding the right words.

Ever since the sixteenth-century, we have tried to pray in public using one of two patterns: free prayer or set prayer. All that could possibly be said about the relative merits of either was said in seventeenth-century controversies. In favor of free or extempore prayer it was argued that it had the merits of spontaneity and relevance. It showed trust in the presence and help of the Holy Spirit and yet relied on the minister's sensitivities to articulate the concerns of his people. Those preferring set prayer stressed the wider range of experience in prayers coming from many peoples and times and the freedom from idiosyncrasies and whims.

Both forms had drawbacks. Free prayers, at their best, were apt articulations of the cries of men's spirits. At the worst, they were limited, narrow, and repetitive. Set prayers could widen the horizon of men's concern by the catholicity of experience they offered. But they too could be alien phrases droned on in vain repetition.

The problem we face in prayer today is present in both types. In either case, we learned to pray in the past whether with free forms or set ones. We have imbibed so thoroughly past concepts of how to pray that we are scarcely prepared to pray in our time. Ironically, those accustomed to free prayer are more firmly fixed in their ways than those who practice the use of set forms that can be replaced by other set forms. The former has to refashion his whole creativity, the other can let someone else help him. It may well be that free forms are in danger of becoming the more rigid of the two methods.

How real to most Christians is the sense of direct divine providence that our prayers presuppose? Are we praying in a context of genuine trust when we petition God to see to this and that? Do we really pray "yet not my will but thine be done," as ready to accept a "no" as a "yes"? As we voice our shopping list of petitions each Sunday, we wonder how seriously most Christians take the possibility of God acting through us, without us, or in spite of us. Are intercession and petition simply empty exercises for congregations who hardly expect to unleash an angel or two? We wonder. Are we really so confident in prayer as we have sounded in the past?

Or again, is it possible for modern man to voice praise to God? The only time we offer praise of persons today is in nominating speeches at political conventions, and even the most fervent partisan does so with tongue in check. Praise is no longer a familiar form of public speech, and even funeral eulogies have gone sour on us. It is difficult, maybe impossible, for modern man to offer praise in the way he once could when a king represented a whole people.

Our entire tradition of prayer has been largely a celibate one. This is not surprising when we consider the monastic development of the divine office and contributions to the mass. But how often are we accustomed to thank God for the most basic structure of society, the family? We never thank him in public for one of his greatest gifts, that of sexuality. Our language of thanksgiving is curiously stunted. We can wax eloquent about God's gifts in biblical times but grow strangely mute when it comes to gratitude for life, for children, for friendships. And when do we give thanks for the structures of society and the orders of creation by which our lives are daily sustained? It is not surprising that only one of the ten lepers turned back to thank Jesus. We are always forgetting to say "thank you" for what matters most. We have learned to give thanks for a cloistered part of our lives but rarely for the great realities of life.

These are only sample problems of knowing how we ought to pray. Obviously they go far deeper than the form of words we use. Simply updating the words and images will not do. And whether we are accustomed to free forms or rejuvenated set forms, the problems will not go away until we have reconsidered the content of prayer as well as the forms. Obviously some drastic changes are needed if we are to voice the concerns of modern man speaking to his God. We have to learn a new way of thinking before we write contemporary prayers.

This will not be easy and we cannot hope to do more here than offer a few tentative suggestions The changes in form may be obvious, but what really counts is that the content be relevant too. In the best of the new prayers the changes in content may be more striking—even shocking—than the fact that they are in modern speech. We can learn much by looking at some of the provisional efforts being made with regard to both the form and content of prayer. In many cases it is difficult, if not impossible, to distinguish between form and content.

II

Any resolutions of our problems at this point must be highly tentative. The best we can do is to offer a few suggestions and point to some emerging models. This must be more vague and indefinite than chronicling past history, but we can examine a few developments concerning the words of worship that commend themselves to our attention.

The first thing that has become obvious is the impossibility of standard wording for everyone. The day, when by Act of Parliament "all the whole realme shall haue but one use," seems irretrievably past. Modern society is much too varied, too rich, and too heterogeneous for a single language of worship to satisfy everyone. When one considers the varieties of technical languages used today plus the jargons of the various subcultures, the possibility of a satisfactory single liturgical language seems remote. We would hardly expect the black churches to relish the language of the middle-class white church at worship. And the youth have an argot of their own which is fiercely private. By the time their phrases are grasped by the adult population, they have lost their appeal to the youth. Advertising pulls us in yet another direction with its glamorous adjectives. Cranmer sought one liturgical language for the whole realm. We seek many.

We may start with a standard liturgical language, but it will need adaptation for best use by differing groups—children, youth, adults. This is further complicated by the fact that even within the various subcultures change is constant. The idea of a prayer book lasting thirty years, let alone three hundred, seems increasingly absurd. One can think of dozens of words such as "reentry" that have gained new meanings in the last dozen years. Whatever we publish will have to be revised for various groups at intervals.

It would seem that free prayer would be the answer since it is so adaptable. But experience shows that this is often the most stilted form of prayer unless the minister is forced to realize the limitations of his concerns and language and seeks wider experience. A deliberate effort to speak the languages of differing groups has to be made without any sense of patronizing or talking down. It takes real sensitivity to lead in prayer those groups whose age or background is dissimilar from our own.

Even the most deliberate effort at being up-to-date will prove a liturgical impossibility. A language becomes common, even in a close group, by reiteration. Words and phrases become familiar by repetition. Advertising depends on this. Gibberish about putting a tiger in our tank sold us gasoline in the 1960's through constant repetition. This suggests that there will inevitably be a certain time lag in the language of worship within each group. Only by reiteration do we develop a common language for praying. Introducing new phrases as rapidly as they develop may render the language less common rather than more so.

Our second suggestion is that we consider some criteria for good liturgical prose. It seems that such criteria could profit from those characteristic of good written prose in our own post-Hemingway day. These qualities seem to revolve around simplicity and clarity. Other ages may have preferred elegance and grace; we are irritated if the meaning is not immediately clear. Our approach to prose is a utilitarian one. We relish a down-to-earth directness that is simple and honest. "Tell it like it is" was a slogan a few years ago and this sums it up well. Be simple, be clear.

Above all, our age abhors overwriting. Anything that reeks of a purple passage seems offensive. An overuse of alliteration, exaggerated metaphors and similes, or anything cute makes us impatient. Our speech prides itself on being natural rather than affected. Prayers seem especially susceptible to temptations of affection and unnaturalness. "Less is more" in writing as well as in architecture. Know when to stop.

Archaisms delighted our Victorian ancestors. They turn us off. Modern writers blue-pencil the occasional whims to reverse the usual succession of verb and noun, to use obsolete words no matter how picturesque, or to employ anything quaint. Our speech is of the here and now, not a languid recalling of days of ere. If the dictionary says "archaic" after a word, scratch it quickly.

In short, modern prose seems to be primarily utilitarian in making its first concern the conveyance of the author's meaning, and in considering entertainment through elegance a minor consideration. One might almost say that the best prose style is one where we are not conscious of any. We want to be conscious of the content but not of the form. Good modern prose serves the reader rather than impresses him. Like good church music and architecture, it is subservient to its function. It does not call attention to itself.

In the third place, we can get some "help and furniture" (to be archaic) by looking at good recent examples of liturgical prose as models to be studied and imitated with discretion. We have already mentioned the new biblical translations, particularly *The Jerusalem Bible* and *The New English Bible.* Both of these provide good contrasts with previous translations and help us discover the direction of modern prose style.

We must take seriously the work of the various liturgical translators and revisers. Some of them have been able to develop fairly systematic procedures in their efforts to create a modern English language of worship. Undoubtedly the International Committee on English in the Liturgy has had the greatest amount of experience with translation. This is a Roman Catholic group with representatives from eleven English-speaking countries around the world. Its responsibility is to translate each *editio typica* of the Catholic liturgical books as the Latin versions are completed in Rome. I.C.E.L. has probably spent more time in considering the qualities of contemporary English liturgical prose than any other group. Its accomplishments, already evident in the new missal, parts of the ritual, and pontifical have been a major factor in making it impossible for any denomination to consider retaining sixteenth-century English in new revisions. The I.C.E.L. translations deserve to be studied as models of clarity and simplicity. They are not contemporary Cranmer and will hardly be regarded as literary masterpieces by future generations. The missalette can be picked up in most Catholic churches in

America and reflects the success of I.C.E.L. in creating an English liturgical prose style worthy of study.

More directly useful are the products of several ecumenical efforts. The Consultation on Common Texts is a group representing the churches in the Consultation on Church Union, Lutherans, and Roman Catholics in this country. These scholars have worked with English liturgical scholars and the I.C.E.L. group in a committee known as the International Consultation on English Texts. From this have come texts of commonly used items such as the Lord's Prayer, the Apostles' and Nicene Creeds, *Te Deum, Sursum Corda,* and various other items.[5] Some of these have already found their way into the Roman mass, the trial Episcopal Communion service, and the Consultation on Church Union's "An Order of Worship." They are worthy of use by all denominations.

Additional models can be found in the new liturgies published by various denominations in recent revisions. These are available in a paperback book entitled *Word & Action*.[6] Another useful collection, the work of the Church of England Liturgical Commission, is a paperback entitled *Modern Liturgical Texts*.[7] Many of these materials are worthy of imitation, particularly as they show efforts to develop contemporary liturgical prose styles, some more conservative than others. As other liturgical revisions are completed, we will have further examples. Especially worth mentioning is the accomplishment of three Presbyterian churches in *The Worshipbook-Services*.[8] The language of this book provides the best model currently available.

There is another type of book that may be even more important. These books, by individual writers, provide models of prayer that are new and challenging both as to content and form. Some of these are explicitly directed to special subcultures and speak the language of definite groups. These may not reflect the way we speak, but overhearing the prayers of those unlike us can force us to reconsider the content of our own. Carl F. Burke is a prison chaplain who has worked

---

[5] For these texts, see *Prayers We Have in Common*, pp. 5-23.
[6] John C. Kirby, ed. (New York: Seabury Press, 1969).
[7] (London: S.P.C.K. Press, 1968).
[8] (Philadelphia: Westminster Press, 1970).

with underprivileged children in the city. His two paperback collections, *Treat Me Cool, Lord* and *God Is for Real, Man*[9] are compositions by these children and a witness to everyone. Perhaps better known is the paperback book of Malcolm Boyd, *Are You Running with Me, Jesus?*[10] It reflects the language of a youth culture and sounds more foreign to many of us than Cranmer. But the contents is a striking compilation of the Godward concerns of modern man and worth pondering.

Far less striking stylistically is a valuable paperback volume, *Prayers*, by Michel Quoist.[11] Every pastor should know it. These prayers cannot be used in public worship, but they articulate so well how we can pray today that the book ought to be read and studied carefully. There are several unofficial collections by Catholics that are full of creativity both in style and in content. We may mention several of these: *Eucharistic Liturgies* edited by John Gallen, S.J.;[12] *The Underground Mass Book*, a paperback edited by Stephen W. McNierney; [13] and Robert F. Hooey's paperback, *Experimental Liturgy Book*.[14] Many have found the writings of Louis Evely wonderful sources of meditation, especially his paperback, *That Man Is You*.[15] Two notable Protestant collections are *Contemporary Prayers for Public Worship* and the even better *More Contemporary Prayers*, both edited by Caryl Micklem.[16]

Undoubtedly best of all is a collection by a Dutch ex-priest, Huub Oosterhuis, *Your Word Is Near*,[17] and a more recent volume, *Prayers, Poems and Songs*.[18] Obviously the translator(s) is a gifted man as well. Oosterhuis' book can be used well in public worship, but it ought also to be read in private to help us learn how we ought to pray. The language is handled with the skill of a consummate poet and the content is new, fresh, and provocative. Quoist and Oosterhuis provide the best recent

[9] C. F. Burke, ed. (New York: Association Press, 1968 and 1967).
[10] (New York: Avon Books, 1967).
[11] (New York: Sheed & Ward, 1963).
[12] (New York: Herder and Herder, 1969).
[13] (Baltimore: Helicon, 1968).
[14] (New York: Herder and Herder, 1969).
[15] (New York: Paulist Press, 1967).
[16] (London: S.C.M. Press, 1967 and 1970).
[17] (New York: Newman Press, 1968).
[18] (New York: Herder and Herder, 1970).

collections of prayers, and those of Oosterhuis are in a style that can be used in either public or private worship.

The problems of the words of worship in prayer will not be solved simply by the study of such models, but they can be a major force in priming the pump. Learning to pray as modern men takes a major effort on the part of all who lead public worship. Undoubtedly many will simply be content to update the language and assume that they have solved the problem. While we would not deny that this is a step forward, it is only the beginning of advance on a problem that involves not only our theology but our whole outlook on life. Studying the best recent collections on prayer can help us move ahead further.

It goes without saying that one can hardly expect to be relevant and cogent in leading public prayer if he is not constant in private prayer. New developments tend to emphasize the role of free prayer, making new demands on the pastor's ability to lead in prayer in public. It ought to be presupposed that he practices private prayer on a disciplined daily basis. This is particularly important when shared with another person whose sensitivities to life may stretch his own. Two are more apt to know where the world is hurting than one and also can find more in which to rejoice. If effective public prayer depends upon serious private prayer, then the converse is also true. We pray with best understanding as individuals when our concerns have been rounded out by prayer in the congregation.

Prayer, we are convinced, must be as relevant as preaching. Preaching and prayer are the two parts of most worship services that can be prepared weekly with the immediate situation of the congregation in mind. They are the two parts of worship most directly adaptable to the here and now. And though set prayers remain an important part of worship, it seems likely that all western churches, Roman Catholic and Protestant, are moving to realization of the need for both set prayer and free forms. The words of the sermon in which God's word to us is expounded are balanced by the words of prayer we address to God. Both reflect the timeliness and relevance of the present.

Though prayer must be as relevant as preaching, we must

be careful not to confuse the two. Prayer is vocative not didactic. The Reformers often made this mistake in using prayer as a sermonette. God does not really need a lesson on theology, though many prayers, both Catholic and Protestant, have hinted at that. Prayer is address to God and not to men. It is relevant in offering to him the needs, concerns, and joys of us all. It is a joyful and sorrowful unburdening of ourselves to "You, God" and not a thinly disguised sermon.

Some forms of prayer have become increasingly common in both Protestant and Catholic worship in recent years. There is nothing new about them. They are indeed ancient, though we may be unfamiliar with them. The first is the bidding prayer where the minister asks the congregation to pray for a series of concerns, leaving moments of silence after each bid so the people can formulate their own prayers on the same topic. Sometimes the minister sums up these silent prayers after each silence with a collect and then bids us pray for the next concern. Litanies are familiar to most of us. The minister voices petitions and the people make a response to each with a refrain such as, "Hear us, we beseech thee, O Lord," or more recently: "O God, be our strength," or "Give peace in our time, O Lord." New petitions can be composed weekly.

Increasingly popular is a form of open-ended prayer where the petitions are voiced by members of the congregation. This demands a certain security on the part of the pastor, because no one may be moved to voice a concern on certain occasions whereas on others the time may run long. In some large churches it has been necessary to set up microphones in several parts of the nave for this purpose. This method seems to work best when the person offering a concern ends with some formula such as "let us pray to the Lord." Then the entire group joins in a refrain such as "hear us, O Lord" or "let my people go, Lord." This type of prayer has all the possibilities and risks of spontaneity. It is also a good school of prayer for the congregation. This type of prayer is primarily prayer of intercession in which we pray for the church, for those in positions of authority, and for those in need and distress. It does not take the place of prayers of confession, praise, thanksgiving, and offering. Nor is it a substitute for the Lord's Prayer. Prayer of intercession usually occurs best in close association with the offering of our money and services for others.

We are left with the problem the disciples had after years of prayer: "Lord, teach us to pray." Perhaps the first step is in learning how much we need to learn. Beyond that, the next step seems to be growth in awareness of the activity of both God and man in our time. The more sensitive we become to men's needs, the better we are enabled to pray. But it also seems true that the more we pray, the more open we may become to men's needs. Perhaps we can begin by confessing that we do not know how to pray as modern men and then go on doing it with confidence that the Spirit is on our side.

What we say in prayer or in any other part of worship is most important, but we cannot neglect how we say it either. How we say it will determine how it is heard by our fellow worshipers. Style is important too. We need to learn both new forms and new content for prayer, so we can offer worship in ways natural to man of the 1970s.

INDEX

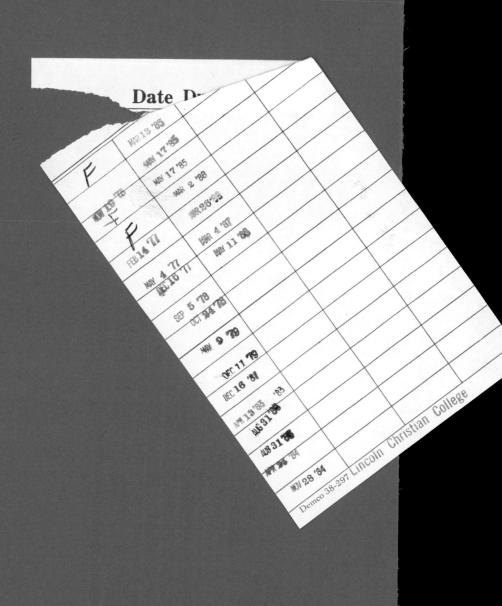

Date Due